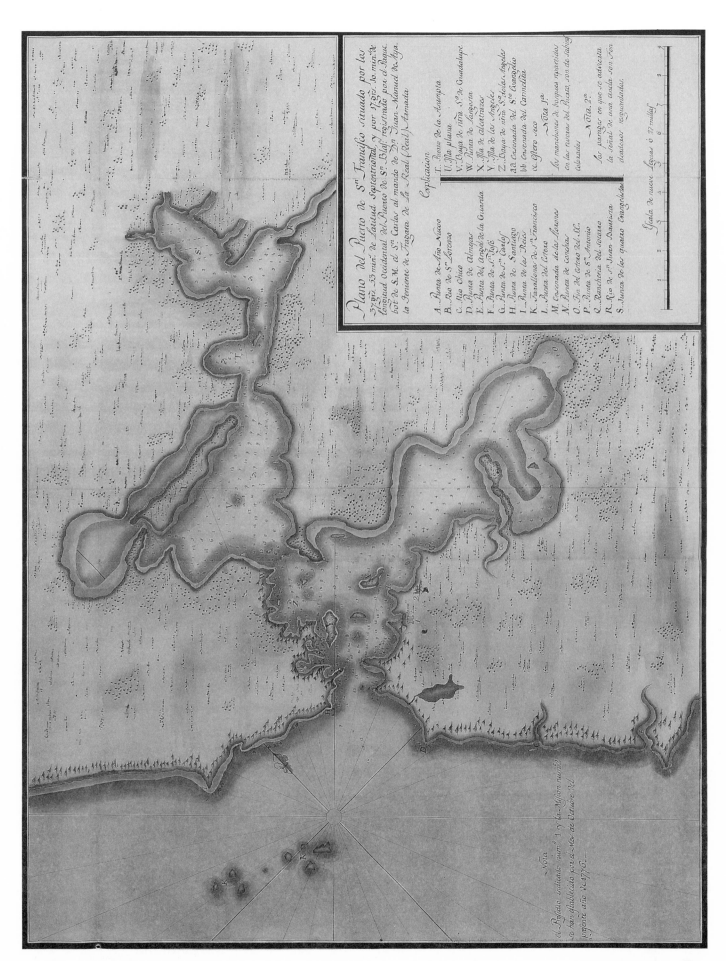

Plano del Puerto de Sn Francisco situado por los
37 grs 53 min. de Latitud Septentrional y por 17 grs. 30 min. de
longitud occidental del Puerto de Sn Blas registrado por el Paquebot de S.M. el Sn Carlos al mando de Dn Juan Manuel de Ayala
la Teniente de Fragata de La Real (Real) Armada

Explicacion

A. Punta de Año-Nuevo
B. Rio de Sn Lorenzo
C. Año Chico
D. Punta de Almejas
E. Punta del angel de la Guarda
F. Punta de Sn Josef
G. Punta de Sta Cardy
H. Punta de Santiago
I. Punta de los Reies
K. Farallones de Sn Francisca
L. Punta del Cetreo
M. Ensenada de los Lovonos
N. Punta de conchas
O. Fin del estero del SC.
P. Punta de Sn Antonio
Q. Rancheria del oceano
R. Rio de Sn Juan Bautista
S. Juera de los quatro Evangelistas

T. Bueno de la Asumpta
U. Isla plana
V. Baxa de otra Sta de Guadalupe
W. Punta de Langosta
X. Isla de alcatrazes
Y. Isla de los Angeles
Z. Baya de otra Sta de los Angeles
aa. Ensenada del Sto Evangelio
bb. Ensenada del Carmelita
cc. Estero seco

Nota 1a
los manchones de buques repartidos
en las rucvas del Puerto, son de sabzzg
alvazados

Nota 2a
las parajes en que se advierta
la señal de una ancla son fon
deaderos resguardados

Grada de nueve Leguas ò 27 millas

Nota
el Puerto indicado num.º 1 y la Mision num.º
se han establecido por el Mes de Octubre del
presente año de 1776.

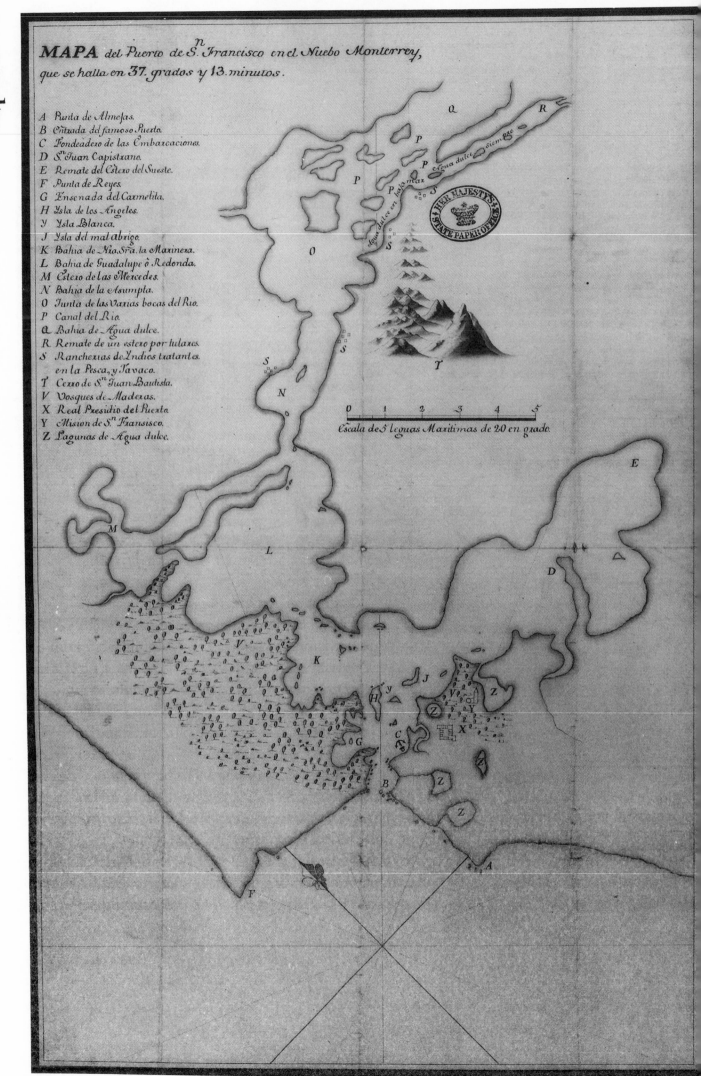

MAPA del Puerto de S.ⁿ Francisco en el Nuebo Monterrey, que se halla en 37. grados y 13. minutos.

A Punta de Almejas.
B Entrada del famoso Puerto.
C Fondeadero de las Embarcaciones.
D S.ⁿ Juan Capistrano.
E Remate del Estero del Sueste.
F Punta de Reyes.
G Ensenada del Carmelita.
H Ysla de los Angeles.
Y Ysla Blanca.
J Ysla del mal abrigo.
K Bahia de N.^{ra} S.^{ra} la Marinera.
L Bahia de Guadalupe ò Redonda.
M Estero de las Mercedes.
N Bahia de la Asumpta.
O Junta de las varias bocas del Rio.
P Canal del Rio.
Q Bahia de Agua dulce.
R Remate de un estero por tulares.
S Rancherias de Indios tratantes.
   en la Pesca, y Tavaco.
T Cerro de S.ⁿ Juan Bautista.
V Vosques de Maderas.
X Real Presidio del Puerto.
Y Mision de S.ⁿ Fransisco.
Z Lagunas de Agua dulce.

Escala de 5 leguas Maritimas de 20 en grado.

THE

MAPS

OF SAN FRANCISCO BAY

from the Spanish Discovery in 1769
to the American Occupation.
By Neal Harlow

The Book Club of California

1950

This reprint is strictly limited to 300 copies

ISBN 1-888262-95-8

Maurizio Martino
472 Howard Avenue
Staten Island, NY 10301

❧❧❧❧❧❧ CONTENTS ❧❧❧❧❧❧

[iv]

[v]

{ *Map No. 28, page* 79 }
Eugène Duflot de Mofras, 1844. *Port de San Francisco.* The Beechey chart translated and revised by Duflot de Mofras.

{ *Map No. 29, page* 80 }
Eugène Duflot de Mofras, 1844. *Entrée du Port de San Francisco.* Accompanies above chart and from same source.

THE MAPS OF THE TOWN OF SAN FRANCISCO, 1835-1847

{ *Map No. 30, page* 83 }
William Antonio Richardson, 1835. [Preliminary sketch of a plan of the town of Yerba Buena.] MS. First plan of the town, made in May 1835.

{ *Map No. 31, page* 85 }*
William Antonio Richardson, 1835. [Plan of Yerba Buena.] MS. First official map of the town, drawn in October 1835.

{ *Map No. 32, page* 87 }
Jacob Primer Leese, 1839? [Plan of Yerba Buena.] MS. Showing the town lots granted to Leese and Salvador Vallejo, 1839.

{ *Map No. 33, page* 90 }*
Jean Jacques Vioget, 1839. *Plan of Yerba Buena.* MS. The first map from an actual survey.

{ *Map No. 34, page* 92 }
Anonymous, 1843? [Map of the Town of Yerba Buena.] MS. An enlargement of Vioget's map, with streets at right angles.

{ *Map No. 35, page* 94 }
John Henry Brown, 1846. [Plan of Yerba Buena.] MS. A copy of the "first map of surveyed land."

{ *Map No. 36, page* 96 }*
Washington Allon Bartlett, 1847. *A map of the Town of San Francisco.* MS. The "Alcalde map" of San Francisco.

[vi]

{ *Map No.* 37, *page* 98 }
Jasper O'Farrell, 1847. [Map of San Francisco.] MS. Map of the first modern survey of the town, made under American auspices.

{ *Map No.* 38, *page* 101 }
Jasper O'Farrell, 1847. [Map of the beach and water lots of San Francisco.] MS. O'Farrell's survey of the tide lots along the waterfront of the town, prepared for the public sale in July 1847.

{ *Map No.* 39, *page* 103 }*
Jasper O'Farrell, 1847. [The original and authentic plan of San Francisco, enlarged and drawn from the latest actual surveys.] A map combining the several surveys of the town made by O'Farrell.

*The asterisk denotes that a reproduction of that map is to be found at or near the page indicated.

Introduction

"I can at least give briefly . . . the news that the harbor of San Francisco is one of the best that I have seen in these seas from Cape Horn northward."

This quotation from Captain Juan Manuel de Ayala's letter of November 9, 1775, to Antonio Maria Bucareli, Viceroy of New Spain, accompanied the first official report and map made from a survey, however sketchy, of the bay subsequently described as large enough "to hold all the ships of Spain" or "all the navies of the world."

Neal Harlow's The Maps of San Francisco Bay from the Spanish Discovery in 1769 to the American Occupation *was published in 1950 by The Book Club of California and printed in San Francisco by the Grabhorn Press. Lauded by the publisher as "a definitive work on the subject, one of permanent importance to historians, scholars and collectors of Californiana," the handsomely printed and illustrated work has stood the test of time. A new limited-edition reprint by Maurizio Martino Fine Books is now welcome, for the original edition of only 375 copies has become increasingly difficult to acquire.*

In an article appearing in the Winter 1950 issue of the Quarterly News-Letter *of The Book Club of California, Harlow described the genesis of this work. His interest developed when he was living in San Francisco and working at the Bancroft Library of the University of California, Berkeley. The commute was by ferry, as this was before the San Francisco-Oakland Bay Bridge was completed. In Harlow's own words: "Riding the old ferry boats, with a stong chill wind on the foredeck and a squawking pack of querulous gulls attacking and boarding at the rear, I acquired an interest in the San Francisco Bay and its maps. . . ." The book reprinted here was one outcome of that developing interest in cartography and history. It was followed by his fine cartobibliographic works on the early maps of Los Angeles* (Maps and Surveys of the Pueblo Lands of Los Angeles, 1976) *and of San Diego* (Maps of the Pueblo Lands of San Diego, 1987), *as well as a riveting history of the American conquest of Alta California* (California Conquered: War and Peace on the Pacific, 1982).

Harlow's 1950 work, with an elegant historical account of the explorations of the coast and the bay, descibes and analyzes the twenty-nine maps he could find for the time frame delimited in the title. That his research was meticulous and comprehensive is suggested by the paucity of maps that have surfaced in the succeeding forty-six years. In the addenda to this reprint are the only two additional maps found during a period in which eager eyes, both amateur and professional, have sought new finds and worldwide interest in historical cartography has heightened immeasurably. One of the two maps in the addenda is a Spanish manuscript chart I discovered in England in the Public Records Office, Kew. Harlow acknowledged the existence of this chart in his commentary on Map No. 12, entitled "Plan of Port San Francisco in New Albion . . . from a Spanish Ms. [London, 1790]." Harlow notes: "If the chart was a true copy, the 'Spanish Ms.' was a curious source, and its identity is not known."

The Book Club of California had then, and possesses to this day, a reputation for publishing significant works of California history and fine printing. The Club's first book, published in 1914, was Robert Cowan's A Bibliography of the History of California and the Pacific West, 1510–1906, *still often cited and reprinted three times by others. Ten percent of The Book Club's more than 200 publications to date are of significant cartographic interest, including Harlow's 1950 work, which is BCC 77 in the chronological listing. Others have included Robert Becker's two major works reproducing the early sketch maps known as* diseños, *required as exhibits to accompany applications for Spanish and Mexican land grants in California (BCC 118, 1964, and BCC 133, 1969) and John Leighly's* California as an Island *(BCC 141, 1972).*

The Book Club of California offered Harlow's work to its members for $30 with a pre-publication price of $26.50 (substantial prices for a book in 1950), along with a strong suggestion from the publications committee that members place their orders "promptly, before the edition is fully subscribed." The original was described as a work of extraordinary typographical beauty. A folio of 154 pages, it was printed on Van Gelder paper from Holland, in two colors, and bound in decorated boards and leather back. Copies today occasionally are offered for sale at nearly thirty times the original price.

The Grabhorn brothers are acknowledged to have been among the finest printers in San Francisco, a city with a national reputation for that fine art. The bibliographic listing of books bearing the Grabhorn Press label contains 654 entries dating from 1916 to 1965. All but the first thirteen were printed in San Francisco, commencing with GB 14 in 1921. Harlow's The Maps of San Francisco Bay is GB 501. An important scholarly work, finely printed and in limited edition, could not help but attract the attention of collectors of publications of The Book Club of California and the Grabhorn Press. Until now, those interested in historical cartography often have been frustrated by the cost and scarcity of the volume.

In 1994 Warren Heckrotte prepared for members of the California Map Society a list of eighteen books of significance for the early mapping of California. A nineteenth must now be added: the much expanded 1995 checklist of the maps of California as an Island by Glen McLaughlin and Nancy H. Mayo. Of these nineteen, Harlow is the author of three; only Carl I. Wheat, with five entries, exceeds that number. Maurizio Martino Fine Books has previously reprinted two of those works by Wheat.

Historical cartography and exploration are inticately intertwined, and in many works the former is overshadowed by the accounting of historical events. Harlow gracefully separates the two in a prefatory overview of cartographic developments and an introductory historical account. His intoduction is a magnificent summary of the explorations associated with the maps, ranking with that of historians such as Charles E. Chapman, Herbert Eugene Bolton, and John W. Caughey. As does Harlow, those authors all acknowledge the contributions of Hubert Howe Bancroft in preserving much of the primary source material.

The volume includes maps of San Francisco Bay produced from 1769 to 1847 on a scale large enough to contribute to topographic knowledge. In his preface Harlow notes that maps of the bay prior to the American conquest are mainly of two cartographic strains, Spanish and English in origin. The Spanish line begins with a chart made in 1775 by José de Cañizares during the first regular survey of the bay and amended by him the following year. The other family of bay maps begins with the plan made by the English expedition under Frederick William Beechey, which visited San Francisco in 1826 and again in 1827–1828. The first two maps listed and reproduced are a coastal chart made by Miguel Costansó in 1770, the first to show the recently discovered bay, and a crude repre-sentation by Juan Crespí in 1772, the first separate map of the bay. Appended to the twenty-nine bay maps are ten maps of the town of San Francisco made from 1835 to 1847, which Harlow describes as a separate category "*intimately related by history as they picture the development of the site fronting upon the most popular place of anchorage in the bay.*"

Harlow's professional training and career prepared him well for both this and his later works. He served initially on the staff of the Bancroft Library, where his interests in cartography and history were nourished. From there he moved to the California State Library, where he worked in Special Collections, and to the Library of the University of California, Los Angeles, where he was assistant librarian under Lawrence Clark Powell. Later he was head librarian at the University of British Columbia and then dean of the Graduate School of Library Service, Rutgers University, until his retirement in 1969. His Maps and Surveys of the Pueblo Lands of Los Angeles *and* Maps of the Pueblo Lands of San Diego, 1602–1874, *also in limited editions, were handsomely printed by Grant Dahlstrom and The Castle Press in Pasadena. Together with the work reprinted here, they form a trilogy of exceptionally fine works of historic cartography of three great cities in California.*

When I approached him with the idea of reprinting the 1950 volume updated with the two additional maps, he graciously agreed, with the observation that the important thing was "to get it right." He has always done so, and we have made every effort here to maintain his standards of excellence. This facsimile edition helps preserve the heritage he has so well documented for us and makes more widely available an important cartobibliographic work.

Alfred W. Newman
Vallejo, California
President, California Maps Society, 1993–1996

HISTORICAL MAPS *are not isolated documents issued for the amusement of bibliographers, but they fall into our hands after their best days are done. If we make a meticulous list of their titles, we record little more than the bare facts of their existence— we compile, as it were, only their vital statistics. Every serious map is a product of circumstances over which some degree of control is sought and exerts a force in shaping events within its scope. By recognizing a map's fundamental utility, we restore its natural dignity and demonstrate its importance as historical evidence.*

In world history San Francisco Bay was a late discovery, but knowledge of its existence runs back to the earliest settlement of California. First encountered by accident, its significance unknown, the bay penetrated far into the land and effectively cut off the explorers' approach to Point Reyes. Even after its importance was recognized, it remained throughout the Spanish and Mexican regime ever subordinate to the position of Monterey as official capital and port. But what in the ease of possession Spain and Mexico so lightly esteemed, foreigners more quickly appreciated, and the bay became the object of many covetous eyes. Guarded then anxiously by its owners, San Francisco was nevertheless visited, soon frequented, and at last acquired by people from other lands. As the harbor begat commerce, so it required maps which, having served their original purpose, often survived to mark a none too well defined route into the past.

Maps of the bay prior to the American conquest prove to be

Preface

mainly of two cartographic strains, Spanish and English in origin. Both were prolific and produced laterals in several languages. Other maps appeared but lacked essential regenerative power. The founder of the Spanish line was a chart made by José de Cañizares aboard the San Carlos during the initial survey in 1775. Amended by him in 1776, it was improved slightly by Josef Camacho in 1779 and touched off a notable succession: the printed Cañizares chart of 1781; a hypothetical manuscript of about 1785; the first printing of the 1785 chart by Dalrymple in London, 1789; a second and more faithful reproduction of it in the atlas to the Voyage de LaPérouse, 1797; and a belated printing of the same source by the Mexican government in 1825; to which may be added the 1790 Dalrymple chart, like and yet dissimilar to its predecessors of 1775, 1776, and 1779.

At the head of the other family of bay maps was the plan made by the English expedition under Frederick William Beechey which visited San Francisco in 1826 and again in 1827-1828. It was followed by a number of manuscript and printed charts associated with this expedition or issued by the British government, and new generations were in time reared by English, French, Russians, and Americans until all were at last superseded by the definitive series of bay charts produced by the United States Coast Survey.

Independent maps by Crespi (that first curious pictograph), Font, Vancouver, and Arrillaga, by the professional pilots of the Naval Department of San Blas, and by Dupetit-Thouars lend interest if not direction to cartographic development. The appended maps of the town of San Francisco, 1835-1847, comprise a separate category but are intimately related by history as they picture the development of the site fronting upon the most popular place of anchorage in the bay.

The catalog includes the maps of San Francisco Bay produced during the period from 1769 to 1847 — separate maps depicting the bay on a large enough scale to contribute to topographic knowledge. While the earliest such map appeared in 1772, it has been prefixed here by Miguel Costansó's Carta reducida of 1771, the first chart of the coast to incorporate the new-found bay. Omitted from the study are manuscript diseños, accompanying Spanish and Mexican land grants in the area; these are sufficiently numerous and homogeneous to merit separate listing. 1847 has been chosen as the terminal date because it was a transition year between the end of the Mexican regime in 1846 and the formal acquisition of the country by the United States in 1848. The new era in government, population, and communication was to alter mapping needs and methods.

Items in the catalog are arranged chronologically according to the date appearing upon the face of the map, if one is specified, otherwise by the year the expedition responsible for the map visited San Francisco Bay. Maps which were essentially reprints, such as those in editions of the LaPérouse Voyage (which expedition did not enter the bay), are assigned the date of their publication. Bibliographic symbols have been kept to a minimum: three dots indicate the omission of words from a title, and brackets show that material has been supplied. The capitalization of map

Preface *titles in the catalog follows standard library practice; upper and lower case characters were often used indiscriminately by the cartographers, and it is not always possible to distinguish between the two types of letters. Dimensions, as far as possible, are in centimeters, vertical by horizontal, within the maps' innermost borders, computed to the nearest half centimeter; in some instances measurements have been taken from secondary sources and may be given in inches, while occasionally the information has not been available. Following each map entry, references are made to earlier lists in which the map may have appeared. For fuller bibliographic data regarding the sources, consult the bibliography at the end of the book.*

The two-fold purpose of the catalog is to establish clearly each map's identity and to define its position in relation to its historical background. The "Historical Account of the Explorations" which precedes it has arisen naturally from the bibliographic investigations, and should, vice versa, orient the maps to the circumstances which produced them.

Liberal assistance in the preparation of this study has been given by Miss Edith M. Coulter and August Frugé of the University of California, Berkeley, by Francis P. Farquhar, also of Berkeley, and Mrs. Marian Harlow; it is gratefully acknowledged here. Mrs. Eleanor Bancroft, of the Bancroft Library, Miss Caroline Wenzel, of the California State Library, Willis Kerr of Claremont Colleges Library, and other indulgent friends and librarians have given their aid as often as it was needed.

—NEAL HARLOW

HISTORICAL ACCOUNT OF THE EXPLORATIONS

THE modern bay of San Francisco was discovered accidentally by a party of landsmen in 1769 and first placed on a map in 1771. America's finest west coast harbor, it was the last to be discovered. Invisible from the sea in thick weather and virtually camouflaged by the blending hills of the *contra costa* even when clear, San Francisco's Golden Gate remained long unknown. Two and a quarter centuries of previous reconnoitering had disclosed no more promising port in the vicinity than what is now known as Drakes Bay, a dubious though famous little haven under Point Reyes. With this bight, itself named San Francisco in 1595, the new-found harbor was for a time confused, but the great inland bay far outclassed its tiny neighbor and soon usurped both its name and fame.

Upper California, until 1769, lay off the shores of civilization, along the watery edge of a continent. Juan Rodríguez Cabrillo first broke its wild solitude in 1542. His ship passed San Francisco, and land was sighted in the vicinities of Point Reyes and Monterey, but no pause was made nearby.[1] Afterwards, Francis Drake skirted the same coast in mid-1579, labeling it "Nova Albion," and halted in some "faire and good bay" to ready his ship for the arduous Pacific voyage.[2] Pedro de Unamuno explored as far as 39° in 1587 but made no landfalls near San Francisco.[3] Weary seafarers occasionally glimpsed the fancifully charted land from the littered deck of a Manila galleon as it made the final leg of its long eastward run to Mexico. A richly laden ship of this trade left the established route in 1595 to explore the unknown coast, and in a little bay east of Point Reyes (now known as Drakes Bay) met disaster. There on November 7, the captain, Sebastian Rodríguez Cermeño, called the place San Francisco.[4] This small, open bay with its estuary leading into the land was visited and renamed Don Gaspar by Sebastian Vizcaíno in 1603,[5] and his hymn of praise for the nearby port of Monterey impelled Spain's Philip III to urgently recommend its occupation as a way station for the galleon trade.[6] After 168 years the royal will was at last fulfilled and, by chance, the modern bay of San Francisco found. Vizcaíno's Don Gaspar was also to be known as the Puerto de los Reyes, and the harbor of Sir Francisco Drake; but usage would approve San Francisco, the title at last inherited by the more illustrious neighbor.

Spain's recurrent intention to occupy Alta California had repeatedly come to naught, and final settlement in that quarter in 1769 culminated a series of historical events, governed in New Spain to a considerable extent by the will of a single man. José de Gálvez, visitor-general, was sent to Mexico by Charles III in 1765 to overhaul the tax system and treasury and make other investigations peculiar to his office. After effecting the expulsion of the Jesuits, as required by royal mandate, and quelling disorders in the southern provinces, his attention was turned to conditions in the north. There, rebellious Indians had to be subdued, the government of Lower California, lately administered by the Jesuits, reorganized, and decisive steps taken to consolidate and strengthen the far frontier. What precise plan Gálvez had formulated for Upper California is not known, but prior to his arrival at San Blas, on the way to the peninsula, a dispatch from the viceroy ordered that measures be taken to secure California against the Russians. No definite course of action was prescribed, but Gálvez, thus spurred, projected his bold plan to occupy San Diego and Monterey. While rehabilitating the peninsula, the dexterous visitor-general prepared expeditions for the northern coast, commandeering the best ships, supplies and personnel to forward his cherished plan.[7]

Four expeditions from Lower California reached San Diego during the first seven months of 1769, two each by land and sea.[8] At the close of this strenuous journey, some forty men, sick and dying, were established at San Diego while a ship returned to San Blas for supplies and recruits, and the remaining able-bodied members of the party set out under Gaspar de Portolá to rediscover Monterey.[9] Failing in October to recognize Monterey Bay, they continued up the coast, hoping to come upon it, and on October 31, having climbed Montara Mountain which barred their passage along the shore, saw the great Bay of the Farallones before them. Out in the sea were the six or seven small islands, and, breaking the coast line between them and the distant white cliffs of Point Reyes, an estuary made its way into the land. Here they recognized the landmarks of

[4]

what Cermeño named San Francisco,[10] and they then knew Monterey had been passed. José Francisco Ortega and a party of scouts set out next day in the direction of Point Reyes, and on the first of November 1769 found the great inland bay which lay across their path. On November 2, a hunting party reported the same natural wonder, and Portolá was not surprised when Ortega and his explorers returned, unable to reach their destination in the three allotted days.[11]

Portolá expressed only disappointment that Monterey had not been found. Though marvelling at the great extent of the inland bay, he and his men did not understand the import of their discovery. So well did the appearance of the country agree with the description of it which they had read that they believed the bay to be surely "the estuary of which the pilot Cabrera Bueno spoke."[12] Their error was one of degree: they supposed Cermeño's San Francisco at Point Reyes (now Drakes Bay) to encompass the whole open Bay of the Farallones outside the Golden Gate, and Golden Gate Channel was thus mistaken for the diminutive estuary which led inland from Drakes Bay. Thus the new-found bay was for a time called the "Estero de San Francisco," and not until its unique and extraordinary nature was realized did it acquire separate identity.

Before beginning the return journey, a number of Portolá's scouts under Ortega rounded the southern end of the bay and proceeded northward to within sight of San Pablo Bay, dispelling a rumor that a Spanish vessel was anchored in the port. Then marching wearily southward, the party reached San Diego on January 24, 1770.[13]

Monterey was founded on June 3, 1770, and on November 12 of the same year officials in Mexico ordered the establishment of other missions, including one near Point Reyes, at the original harbor of San Francisco. They also required an examination of that harbor, but before the order reached California, Pedro Fages, military commander at Monterey, undertook a volunteer exploration. With seven men he set out from Monterey on November 21, 1770, cut a new trail through the Santa Clara Valley to the southern tip of the "estero," and continued along the east bay shore, exceeding by seven leagues the point reached by Ortega the previous year.

It was of course impracticable to reach Point Reyes by land, and a return was made to Monterey by December 4.[14]

Fages' official orders to explore at Point Reyes reached California in May 1771, but their execution was delayed two months by a lack of supporting troops. Then on March 20, 1772, he with Juan Crespí and a number of soldiers marched northward again along the east bay shore, over the sites of Oakland and Berkeley to Carquinez Strait, where their approach to Point Reyes was still cut off. In the hills near Willows Pass they first viewed the delta of the Sacramento and San Joaquin rivers, and in the vicinity of Antioch christened their new find the Río de San Francisco, "the largest that has been discovered in New Spain." By cross-country the party returned to Monterey on April 4, having added considerably to their knowledge of San Francisco Bay and obtained information from which Crespí produced the first curious map of the bay.[15]

To Captain Rivera y Moncada, who succeeded Fages as governor in August 1773, the viceroy emphasized the urgency of making additional explorations at San Francisco, and when new troops arrived he set out, accompanied by Francisco Palóu and a protective guard. Leaving Monterey on November 23, 1774, he followed Fages' route across the Santa Clara Valley, turning left this time to San Francisquito Creek, then to Lake Merced. Rivera and Palóu followed the beach to the "Cliff" at Point Lobos and were the first to stand on that point. The weather had been rainy and disagreeable, and although an extended exploration of the region had been planned, even to the sources of the rivers if time permitted, Rivera concluded to postpone further action until a more convenient season. The return march to Monterey was by the shore trail of 1769, and having seen only a small portion of the peninsula and had only a glimpse of the bay, the governor reported unfavorably upon the San Francisco project, an attitude he would maintain until 1776.[16]

Plans to occupy San Francisco were fast maturing in Mexico. It was now proposed to establish a presidio there, peopled by soldiers and their families to be escorted overland from Sonora by Juan Bautista de Anza. In preparation for settlement, a supply ship, the *San Carlos*, was assigned to explore the bay, and for the first time interest centered more in the new bay than in the old.

[6]

The *San Carlos*, under Juan Manuel de Ayala, reached Monterey from San Blas on June 29, 1775, and reëmbarked for San Francisco Bay on July 27. Early on August 5, Point San Pedro, south of San Francisco, was sighted, and First Pilot José Cañizares and ten men were dispatched in the ship's boat to locate a place of anchorage. Nearing the Golden Gate, the launch was swept into the bay on a rising tide and was unable to return to the ship as directed. By 8:30 P.M. the *San Carlos* was also in the mouth but beating against a tide which had meanwhile turned. The force of the wind opposing that of the tide threatened the security of the masts, but once the ship had passed Lime Point, the wind calmed and anchor was cast on the north side of the channel, off Richardson Bay. Forty days the vessel remained at San Francisco, and Ayala, who had been seriously injured early in the voyage, placed the work of the survey in Cañizares' hands. A permanent anchorage was found off the northwestern shore of Angel Island, and Cañizares and the second pilot, Juan Bautista Aguirre, took soundings and made observations as far inland as Suisun Bay. The examination was concluded on September 6, and after several abortive attempts to depart, the *San Carlos* sailed out of the gate on the 18th, its course set for Monterey.

The first official survey of modern San Francisco Bay was thus completed, and Cañizares drew up a report and map of his findings.[17] No longer a minor estuary or a water barrier, the new bay was acknowledged to be a separate and great port, "one of the best in all New Spain . . . not one harbor only, but many." Cañizares labeled it the "Puerto de San Francisco" on his chart and, in doing so, entirely ignored the outer bay which had been previously so named. San Francisco need be no more confused with Drakes Bay nor must its settlement await the exploration of the more inaccessible north shore.

In line with Spain's new policy of vigilance on the northwest coast, a series of exploratory voyages was instigated in 1774, to continue for almost two decades. Juan Pérez made the first northward sally in the *Santiago*, sailing from Monterey on June 11, 1774, and ascending to 55° of latitude before returning to Monterey on August 29. He did not enter San Francisco Bay and referred to it only as the "great estuary" yet unnamed.[18] Pérez was followed in

March 1775 by Bruno de Hezeta and Juan Francisco de la Bodega in the *Santiago* and *Sonora*. The latter reached 58°, entered and named Bodega Bay on the return trip, and reached Monterey on September 7.[19] Hezeta took possession at Trinidad and, being prevented by fog from entering San Francisco Bay on August 25, anchored at Monterey on the 29th. Finding that Governor Rivera had not yet sent a land expedition to San Francisco to coöperate with Ayala as ordered by the Viceroy, he immediately collected a party for that purpose. With fathers Palóu and Campa and a military escort, he followed Rivera's route across the Santa Clara Valley and up the peninsula to Point Lobos, where it was soon ascertained that Ayala had departed. Pursuing no new explorations, they named Lake Merced on September 23, and reached Monterey on October 1, after an absence of only seventeen days.[20]

In 1774 Anza had opened the first all-overland route from Mexico to Alta California, and by this strategic desert road he was to escort the colonists to San Francisco. Reaching San Gabriel in January 1776, he was delayed by Rivera to quell an Indian riot at San Diego but proceeded to Monterey at the first opportunity. Still lacking the assistance from Rivera needed to found a colony at the bay, Anza set out from Monterey with a small party on March 23, 1776, to select sites for settlement and thus fulfill at least part of his expiring commission.

With Pedro Font, Gabriel Moraga, and ten soldiers, Anza marched immediately to the peninsula, followed the modern highway route up through the sites of Palo Alto and Daly City, and reached the mouth of the bay on March 27, 1776. The presidio site high on Fort Point was selected on the 28th, after which the expedition turned the southern arm of the bay and followed the base of the hills through Alameda and Contra Costa counties to Carquinez Strait. Font, who was making sketch maps to accompany his diary, supposed this to be Fages' Río de San Francisco of 1772, and at great pains proved it to be no river at all but a fresh water lake. Anza had hoped to cross the valley to the snowy Sierra, but the boggy *tulares* forced the party to go instead along the east side of Mount Diablo, and they came out at Monterey on April 8. As Rivera remained silent regarding the San Francisco establishment,

[8]

Anza intrusted the immigrant families to Moraga and, with Font, set out for Sonora.[21]

Rivera's opposition apparently collapsed after Anza's departure, for on June 17 Moraga and twenty families were on the way to San Francisco. Ten days later the caravan reached the mission site, where a temporary structure was immediately set up. While awaiting the appearance of the *San Carlos*, Moraga surveyed the presidio grounds and, ignoring Rivera's instructions, permitted fathers Palóu and Cambon to begin work on the mission. On August 18, much delayed in passage, the ship anchored below the presidio site and the erection of buildings was started. The presidio was ceremoniously dedicated on September 17, and the completion of the mission was celebrated the following October 9. San Francisco was occupied.

Before the *San Carlos* lifted its anchor on October 21, a new survey of the rivers was undertaken. Fernando Quirós, Cañizares, and Father Cambon in the ship's boat, and Moraga with a land party arranged to meet at Carquinez Strait within three days, where combined operations were to begin. When Moraga, with most of the provisions, failed to appear at the rendezvous, the boat party turned back and on the downward trip explored Petaluma Creek, proving that San Francisco and Bodega bays were not joined. Moraga, who had taken a short cut across the hills, coming out on the river well above the meeting place, made a quick three-day march upstream and another day's journey into the plain before returning to the presidio on October 7. He had been first to penetrate the interior.[22]

Following the Pérez and Hezeta expeditions of 1774 and 1775, a third in the series of Spanish voyages was instigated in Mexico in 1776 in response to news that the Englishman, Captain James Cook, was to be dispatched to the Pacific. Administrative delays, however, held up the departure until a year after Cook's arrival. Setting out in February 1779, Ignacio Arteaga in the *Princesa* and Bodega in the *Favorita* sailed north to 60° and carried out a considerable reconnaissance, particularly in Bucareli Sound. Though not scheduled to stop at San Francisco, they were separated on the return trip and both resorted to the bay. The *Favorita* appeared on the 14th, the *Princesa* on the 15th of September, and before their departure on October 30, the occasion was taken to reëxamine the harbor and the old bay at Point Reyes.[23] The vessels were again at San Francisco in 1782, but were chiefly employed in a survey of the Santa Barbara coast.[24]

With the return of the expedition of 1779, Spanish exploration of the northwest coast was believed to be virtually completed, but the publication in 1784 of the report of Cook's epochal voyage to the Pacific opened up a new era of commerce and exploration.[25] Cook had accidentally discovered that furs secured for a trifle in America were of fabulous value in the Chinese market; and ships from England, the United States, and France quickly entered the new commerce, while Russian participation was assured by the existence in North America of a new base established in 1783. Fortunately for the security of Spanish interests in California, the bulk of this trade was in the beginning confined largely to the coasts far north of San Francisco.[26]

The increased foreign competition brought about a new burst of Spanish activity. Estévan José Martínez and López de Haro investigated Russian advances at Nootka in 1788, fortifying the place and seizing two English vessels there the next year.[27] Eliza, Fidalgo, and Quimper beat up the coast as far as Alaska during 1790 and 1791,[28] and in the latter year Malaspina's round-the-globe expedition visited the north Pacific and stopped at Monterey.[29] The famous ships *Sutil* and *Mexicana* under Galiano and Valdés engaged in a coöperative survey of the Strait of Juan de Fuca with George Vancouver in 1792, while Caamaño made detailed observations beyond Vancouver Island.[30] Bodega y Quadra met Vancouver at Nootka in August 1792 to negotiate a boundary settlement pending under a treaty of 1790 between Spain and England, but Vancouver's view that San Francisco was Spain's northern border was intolerable to the Spanish, and the question was passed back to the home governments for final decision.[31]

California's brief season as an isolated Spanish community was almost ended. The first foreigner to anchor in any California port appeared in 1786, the first at San Francisco in 1792, and others would soon come to poach, smuggle, and snoop along her coastal fringe. Explorers, fur hunters, whalers, hide and tallow traders, merchants, adventurers, and hardy immigrant settlers would gradually effect a penetration of the country. From the first, newcomers would note the unexplored opportunities and predict for California an ultimate change in sovereignty; some would covertly lend a hand to force its unsettled destiny. By reason of its many striking features, San Francisco Bay would ever loom large as an object of foreign aspiration.

In 1786 the Frenchman Jean François Galaup de LaPérouse brought the first foreign vessel to California. Engaged in a round-the-world expedition with instructions to explore and make careful surveys, observing whatever might be turned to the national advantage, he anchored at Monterey on September 15 and was as cordially received by the Californians as if he had been a citizen of their own nation. Taking but limited advantage of the opportunity to make observations and inquiries regarding the country, he did not visit San Francisco and other California ports; the *Boussole* and *Astrolabe* sailed westward on September 24 to suffer the tragic fate meted out to them in the New Hebrides.[32]

George Vancouver performed the next great English voyage to the Pacific after Captain Cook and sailed the first foreign ship into San Francisco Bay. Following up the explorations of his predecessor, and filling in some of the gaps in his survey, he yet hoped to run into the western entrance of an undiscovered northern passage. First sighting the California coast on April 17, 1792, he made extended explorations in the north, where he treated with Bodega y Quadra regarding the Nootka affair before beginning the southern leg of the voyage in October. On November 14 the *Discovery* entered San Francisco Bay, anchoring probably at Yerba Buena but transferring later to the presidio, and was followed by the *Chatham* on the 25th. Vancouver was allowed untrammelled freedom by the Spanish authorities, being taken into the presidio and the missions of San Francisco and Santa Clara. With the exception of the observations made at these establishments, however, he secured but slight information about the harbor, and that at second hand, attributing his failure to the lack of authority to make a regular survey, his haste to meet Bodega at Monterey, and bad weather. He departed for Monterey on October 25, declaring San Francisco to be as fine a port as the world afforded.[33]

Historical Account

Temporary Governor Arrillaga felt considerable personal anxiety over the liberty rashly permitted Vancouver at San Francisco, and he was still more ill at ease when a warning was received from Mexico to guard against foreign vessels, particularly English, on the coast.[34] Again responding to reports of foreign advances in the north, this time by an American, Robert Gray, who had discovered the Columbia River the previous year, the government in Mexico sent out two ships in April 1793 to assess the Spanish interest in the new waterway. Eliza and Martínez y Zayas performed the voyage in the *Activa* and *Mexicana*, and this proved to be the last Spanish expedition to the far north.[35] Closer to California, a new settlement was proposed by the Spanish at Bodega to serve both as a buffer and as a means of forestalling a supposed English seizure of the strategic site. Juan Bautista Matute and Salvador Meléndez arrived there in the *Sutil* and *Aranzazu* in July 1793 but soon abandoned the undertaking and repaired to San Francisco. A road to Bodega was also projected, but a Spanish base never materialized there.[36] Eliza, returning from the north in the *Activa*, accompanied Matute to San Francisco in July and carried out a survey of the bay, leaving for Monterey on September 5.[37] Martínez y Zayas also anchored there from September 17 to October 16 on his homeward voyage.[38]

Vancouver recrossed from the Hawaiian Islands to the California coast in the spring of 1793, again dropping anchor in the bay on October 19. Although courteously received, his movements were this time much restricted, and when the *Chatham* arrived from making a partial survey at Bodega, he sailed for Monterey on the 24th.[39] On the California coast again in 1794, Vancouver this time avoided San Francisco and stopped at Monterey only a short time to obtain supplies and to work on maps and reports.[40]

The expansion of the fur trade toward the south—a movement which would eventually bring Aleut hunters in force into San Francisco Bay—was pioneered by American traders, audaciously flouting Spanish mercantile restrictions to secure their prized cargoes. English and Russians soon followed. Russian incursions into California waters began shortly after the turn of the century, with the dual object of extending the fur fields and supplying essential farm products for the northern settlements. Participating at first through a contract system with American and English vessels, the Russian-American Company began to send down its own ships in 1809 and soon had a firm grip on the southern seal and otter trade.

The Russian far northern base at Sitka was heavily dependent upon imports for its existence, and in 1805, when an imperial inspector found starvation threatening the settlement, he purchased the American ship *Juno* in port and turned its prow toward California. This officer, Nikolai Petrovich Rezánof, fitted the vessel with a tempting lot of merchandise and brought it boldly into San Francisco Bay. Determined to secure produce to succor the Russian colony, he also expected to establish relations which would permanently benefit the company's interests. On April 5, 1806, the Russians—hobgoblin to the Spanish for half a century—sailed past the fort and came to anchor. Until recently Rezánof had been attached to a round-the-world expedition of which the Californians had knowledge, and he was therefore not wholly unexpected at San Francisco, although the peculiar conditions surrounding his appearance required explanation. The story of his intimate relations with Concepción Argüello, fifteen year old daughter of the commandante, is now well known. Whether it was an affair of romance or of state, Rezánof made the best of his close association with the Argüellos. By winning the California governor to his side and seditiously whetting the ready appetites of the padres for the manufactured goods on board the *Juno*, he secured the desired cargo and sailed from the bay on May 21. The expedition's German scientist, Georg Heinrich Langsdorff, had meanwhile succeeded in making some limited investigations about the bay and had visited the missions of San Francisco and San Jose. He obtained hearsay evidence regarding the great rivers to the east and marvelled at the utter lack of water communication.[41]

Rezánof did not live to prove his fidelity to Concepción, but his visit bore fruit. Local commercial relations between the two nations were continued and expanded, and a Russian base bordering on California was soon established, though without Spanish approval. After preliminary observations had been made by the Russians in 1807, 1809, and 1811, a fortified settlement was commenced in 1812 at Ross, north of San Francisco, with a port at nearby Bodega.

Both colony and commerce persisted in the face of Mexican opposition and Californian tolerance until the relationship no longer served the Russian interest.[42]

On October 2, 1816, the Russian vessel *Rurik* entered San Francisco Bay, running down the coast from Bering Strait, where explorations for an Arctic passage to the Atlantic were being pursued. Otto von Kotzebue, the commander, though imperious in manner, was given a friendly welcome. Representatives of the two nations haggled over the removal of the Bodega settlement and signalized their lack of authority to arbitrate the matter by signing a meaningless protocol at the presidio while Russian hunters poached in the bay. The sojourn at San Francisco was brief, terminating on November 1, and the voyage of the *Rurik* is rightly celebrated for the publications prepared by the scientists of the party. The Russians were permitted little freedom of movement: a camp on the beach, numerous visits to the presidio and mission, and one trip to the north shore by the naturalist Chamisso. They were told of two great rivers to the north, and an Indian expedition returned from the Sacramento during their stay. Thorough geographical explorations were of course out of the question—as Chamisso said of their local researches in ethnology and linguistics, these "we must leave . . . to our successors, as our predecessors have done to us."[43]

The first French vessel in San Francisco Bay was the *Bordelais*, a merchantman commanded by Camille de Roquefeuil of the French navy, engaged in a commercial voyage to the Pacific and around the world. Arriving at the Yerba Buena anchorage on August 5, 1817, the party was well received, being of the Catholic faith, visited the presidio and mission and engaged in trade, securing produce and a few furs. Departing for Nootka on August 14, Roquefeuil returned for two other visits, from October 16 to November 2 of the same year and from September 20 to October 20, 1818. He reported an ascent of the "San Sacramento" by Luis Argüello to a distance of fifty leagues, probably in one of the four poorly made boats Roquefeuil had seen at the presidio.[44]

Although the revolutionary movement against Spanish authority in the new world during the first decades of the nineteenth century seethed and boiled explosively, it was known to California only indirectly. The very life blood of the dependent California settle-ments, the annual supply ships, ceased to flow for a number of years, and had it not been for the transfusion of needed goods from foreign vessels on the coast, the situation would have become truly critical. Another local manifestation of the troubled times was the appear-ance in California of two ships under the insurgent Hippolyte Bou-chard. Equipped with letters of marque from the authorities of Buenos Aires to prey upon Spanish commerce, the *Argentina* and *Santa Rosa* were refused aid at Monterey and, in reprisal, harassed the California coast during November and December 1818, making it a winter long remembered as the "año de los insurgentes." Fore-warned, the Californians made warlike preparations from San Fran-cisco to San Diego, but the sheltered harbor at San Francisco was passed unmolested.[45] In 1820 the Californians swore allegiance to the Spanish constitution of 1812, and in April 1822 they as readily recognized the new government of independent Mexico. But the tempo of political affairs in the homeland was too rapid, for Itur-bide's coronation in July 1822 was proclaimed in California the following April, after the new emperor had been deposed. Old time trade restrictions were officially removed by the Mexicans, but like many another action of the superior government, the innovation carried little import in California, where all vessels complying with customs regulations were already welcome.[46]

Eight years after Otto von Kotzebue's first visit to San Francisco he returned on October 8, 1824, this time in the Russian frigate *Predpriatie*. Dispatched as a cruiser to protect the interests of the Russian fur company on the northwest coast, the vessel also carried cargo and a corps of scientists. Hospitably received under the new regime, the visitors made trips to Santa Clara, San Jose, and Ross, and an extended boat voyage up the Sacramento River as far as latitude "38° 37'," perhaps almost to the later site of Sacramento. Anchoring first at the presidio, then at Yerba Buena, they departed on December 6, recording much praise for the natural beauty of the country and no little misinformation.[47]

Among the growing fleet of traders at San Francisco, few of which left published accounts of their visits, was Captain Benjamin Morrell in the American vessel, *Tartar*. On a sealing voyage to the

Historical Account

Pacific, he had visited San Diego and Monterey before anchoring at San Francisco on May 12, 1825. His exaggerated description of the "town of St. Francisco," apparently the presidio community, as containing "120 houses and a church, with perhaps 500 inhabitants," well illustrates Bancroft's contention that "the valiant captain was a liar." Morrell sailed on May 17 for the Sandwich Islands, having concluded it an ill prospect to compete with the Russian fur monopoly.[48]

In 1826, with the appearance at San Francisco Bay of the English expedition under Beechey, the early period of exploration and cartography of the bay came to an end. Since the original survey culminating in the founding of the presidio and mission (and producing the Cañizares charts of 1775 and 1776), two official Spanish explorations had been carried out, one at the time of the Arteaga-Bodega expedition in 1779 (Camacho chart), the other by Eliza in 1793 (the results of which may have been lost). To these may be added the land-based observations of Father Font in 1776 (not widely known), the hydrographic data recorded by Vancouver at the mouth of the bay in 1792, and the manuscript maps (probably closely guarded by the Spanish) compiled about 1803 by the naval pilots at San Blas. A study of the surviving maps reveals that the chart by Cañizares of 1775, modified by him in 1776, and amended but slightly by Camacho in 1779, represented almost the total cartographic data regarding the bay which was generally available at the time of Beechey's arrival in 1826. What was fundamentally Cañizares' work had reappeared in various reincarnations under French, English, and Spanish-Mexican auspices until as late as 1825.[49]

It is interesting to note in regard to land explorations around the bay that the eastern *contra costa*, which had been repeatedly traversed during the opening years of Spanish settlement, soon again became a *tierra incognita*. Vancouver, the first foreign visitor, noted this condition in 1792.[50] In November 1794 mission Indians were sent across to proselyte among the *gentiles*, and the next spring Pedro Amador visited the area called Alameda in his report. A joint expedition from Monterey and Santa Clara headed by Hermenegildo Sal and Raimundo Carrillo explored the Alameda late in 1795; and Mission San Jose was founded on June 11, 1797.[51] Forages by troops in search of mission Indians and marauders both to the north and east of San Francisco Bay repeatedly occurred, accumulating practical experience for the Californians but only haphazard geographical knowledge.[52]

California's Indian fighter and trail-breaker, Gabriel Moraga, may have made an exploration in 1807 from the mouth of the San Joaquin River in the direction of the Sierra Nevada, adding to his observations obtained during several earlier journeys into the lower interior valley.[53] In September 1808 he made his way into the valley near Stockton, searching for mission sites, and there turned northward, exploring toward the headwaters of the Calaveras, Mokelumne, Cosumnes, and American rivers into the Sierra. He crossed the Feather River, which he named the Sacramento, passed the Sutter Buttes, and followed the upper Sacramento for ten leagues, calling it the Jesús María. Returning southward, he explored along the Tuolumne and Merced rivers and came back to San Jose mission.[54] In August and October 1810, Moraga also worked up the San Joaquin River to a point sixty or eighty miles from its mouth.[55] In October 1811 a large party commanded by José Antonio Sanchez set out in boats from San Francisco, headed for the "ríos grandes," and this was probably the first exploratory voyage on the bay since Ayala. They went by way of Angel Island, Point San Pedro, Carquinez Strait, and Suisun Bay and made short excursions into the San Joaquin and Sacramento rivers, the earliest recorded navigation of the latter stream.[56] Another boat trip into the river region occurred between May 17 and 26, 1817, led by Luis Argüello; the party pressed beyond the site of Sacramento, probably first seen at that time, to within ten leagues of the Sutter Buttes.[57] Kotzebue, in 1824, made the first voyage by a foreigner up the Sacramento River, presaging, with Belcher, Sutter, and other early arrivals, an extensive traffic along this inland water route.

On the northern shore of San Francisco Bay, Ayala's expedition of 1775 made the first limited observations. In the following year Quirós and Cañizares took a ship's boat up Petaluma Creek, proving that San Francisco Bay was not connected by water with Bodega.[58] In 1793 it was proposed to open a road to Bodega, where a Spanish settlement was projected, but only preparatory work was done be-

fore the plan was wholly abandoned.[59] Foreign vessels found at
Bodega Bay a convenient anchorage near San Francisco, and the
Russian, Ivan Kuskof, while there in 1809 instituted the portage for
Aleut hunters across the tip of Marin peninsula from Point Bonita
to San Francisco Bay as a practical means of evading the Spanish
authorities.[60] Kuskof made observations preliminary to settlement
at Bodega in 1811, and he returned the next year to establish a
colony there and at Ross.[61] Gabriel Moraga performed the first of
a series of land expeditions into the Bodega country in 1810, returning in 1812, 1813, and 1814, and being followed by Californians,
Russians, and visiting foreigners until the journey became common-
place.[62]

Mission San Rafael was founded in 1817, and Luis Argüello with
Father Payeras explored in that vicinity in 1818 or 1819.[63] What
was popularly known as "Argüello's expedition to the Columbia,"
in 1821, was the most extensive northern exploration made during
Spanish-Mexican times in California. It was sent out by Governor
Sola in October 1821 to ascertain the truth of rumors that foreign-
ers from the indeterminate region known to the Californians as "the
Columbia" had established themselves within the territory claimed
by Spain. Sailing from the San Francisco presidio to Carquinez Strait
on October 21, the party went by land along the eastern slope of the
Coast Range to a point on the Sacramento River near modern
Princeton in Colusa County. Having failed to apprehend the intrud-
ers whom they sought, the expedition turned west along Cortina
Creek, proceeded south to Cache Creek, and continued westerly
along the north side of Mount St. Helena to the site of Cloverdale.
Going on to San Rafael, the return to San Francisco was made, and
the journey was concluded on November 15.[64] Before Mission San
Francisco Solano was founded in 1823-1824, Francisco Castro and
Father José Altimira made a preliminary exploration of the surrounding country, leaving San Francisco on June 25, 1823. Going
to San Rafael, on what is now Petaluma, and through the valleys
of Sonoma, Napa, and Suisun, they chose a site in Sonoma Valley
where the mission was erected.[65] Mariano G. Vallejo attempted to
plant settlements on the northern frontier at Petaluma and Santa
Rosa in 1833;[66] and Governor José Figueroa, who was also inter-

ested in peopling the Mexican-Russian borderland, paid a visit to the northern region in August 1834 with the Híjar-Padrés colonists in mind.[67] With the failure of this ambitious colonizing project, Figueroa's will to see a center of population north of the bay resolved itself into an order for Vallejo to establish a community at Sonoma, which was done in 1835.[68]

Into the bay on November 6, 1826, sailed the English sloop *Blossom*, commanded by Frederick William Beechey, captain in the Royal Navy. Sent to the Pacific to coöperate with the arctic expeditions of captains Parry and Franklin, whenever they should reach the Bering Sea, the ship had spent three months in the far north prior to mid-October, running down to San Francisco at the setting in of the arctic winter. As Beechey had been instructed to make surveys in the Pacific, his men were constantly employed in this business while at San Francisco, and the first thoroughly scientific survey of the bay was made at this time. On December 28, he sailed for the Sandwich Islands, remarking in his journal that the stay in San Francisco Bay had been made tedious by a lack of society and that the fathers' ideas, "like the maps pinned against their walls, bore date of 1772." After a second unfruitful season in Bering Sea the following year, the *Blossom* dropped down the coast to Monterey, left on December 17 for San Francisco to secure a supply of water, and on January 3, 1828, departed for England.

Beechey's survey at San Francisco embraced the whole bay as far inland as the entrance of Carquinez Strait. Blossom Rock was placed on the map, named after Beechey's ship, while Alcatraz (Los Alcatraces), the label which Ayala had attached to modern Yerba Buena Island, was transferred to the rock now bearing that name. Local officials gave every needed assistance and required only that a copy of the resulting chart be delivered to them. The survey was carefully and accurately made, although some error was allowed to creep in with information obtained at second-hand, and it was not superseded until well into the American period.[69]

A new source of wealth was to become the foundation of the country's economy during the succeeding years of the Mexican regime in California. Hides and tallow, commodities in foreign trade from 1823, gradually superseded the dwindling commerce in furs and became firmly established as the leading exports and almost the only media of exchange in the period prior to the American occupation. Essentially an English monopoly until 1826, the trade became widely expanded and was a significant factor in opening up the country to foreigners.[70]

A representative of the new commerce was August Bernard Duhaut-Cilly, who arrived at San Francisco Bay on January 26, 1827, coming from the Sandwich Islands. Anchoring the *Héros* below the presidio, he soon moved to Yerba Buena Cove at the suggestion of William A. Richardson (the same Richardson who, in 1835, became the first resident of the new town of Yerba Buena). As a Frenchman and Catholic Duhaut-Cilly was well received by the padres and had little difficulty negotiating for hides and tallow, visiting each of the bay missions before sailing for Santa Cruz on February 7. He was again at San Francisco from June 17 to July 20, 1827, when he went by land to missions Santa Clara and San Jose, transported hides and tallow from Santa Clara to Yerba Buena in Richardson's sloop, sailed in a long boat up circuitous Sonoma Creek on the way to Sonoma, and visited the ranch of Francisco Castro, near present-day Richmond. He came to Monterey and Bodega again in May 1828, but his business was completed at San Francisco Bay and he did not enter. Duhaut-Cilly was a good observer and wrote an interesting, rather gossipy account, one of the best early day descriptions of the area.[71]

The advent of Jedediah Smith in California was portentous for the Mexican regime, for he was the first to make a crossing of the Sierra Nevada. Smith, a Rocky Mountain Fur Company trapper, first appeared in southern California late in 1826, and in May of 1827 he made a perilous journey over the snowy mountains to reach the Great Basin. He was back in California the following October, and in November and December, on his way north, came to San Francisco under the surveillance of the authorities. He briefly described the topography of the bay in his journal, dined with Captain Beechey aboard the *Blossom*, and set out with his party for the interior. Ordered to make his exit by the most direct route, across the Strait of Carquinez, he instead followed the course of the San Joaquin River to the vicinity of Stockton and proceeded northward along the eastern side of the Sacramento. He observed long before Frémont that the "Buenaventura" River, tributary to San Francisco Bay, descended from the north and did not drain the vast country beyond the Sierra Nevada.[72]

Fur traders of the Northwest Company had brought vessels into California ports as early as 1814, and when their business was acquired by the Hudson's Bay Company in 1821, with it went the interest in west-coast trade. A two-way commerce with California was inaugurated as early as 1828, and the first brigade of trappers made its way into the Sacramento Valley the following year, guided by a former companion of Jedediah Smith. Yearly expeditions were soon to follow, a regular Hudson's Bay Company post was established at French Camp, near the site of Stockton, and the rivers and bay were scoured for furs by seasoned trappers of this and competing companies. The Englishmen, by an agreement with the California governor in 1840, opened a company store at Yerba Buena the next year, but the commercial phase of this promising expansionist movement came to an end with the closing of the San Francisco branch in 1845, and its imperialistic pretensions collapsed in 1846. Meanwhile, enterprising nationals of varying allegiance were becoming increasingly familiar with the approaches to California.[73]

Typical of the fleet of hide traders plying along the coast was the American ship *Alert* under Captain Francis A. Thompson, which dropped anchor at Yerba Buena on December 4, 1835. Ship's boats were sent to Santa Clara and other bay missions, hides were collected, wood and water taken on, and the vessel sailed on December 27. The visit was distinguished from scores of similar expeditions during the years by the presence in the ship's crew of young Richard Henry Dana, whose published account of the voyage made himself and the trade famous.[74]

A sequel to the Beechey visit to San Francisco was the expedition of Sir Edward Belcher, one of Beechey's former officers. Revising the English hydrographic charts of the western coast and Pacific islands, Belcher came to San Francisco to extend his predecessor's observations beyond Carquinez Strait upstream to the head of navigation. Arriving on October 19, 1837, and anchoring his ship at Yerba Buena, the commander first visited Santa Clara mission. Explorations were commenced on the 24th, and the upper limit of observation on the Sacramento was reached on the 30th, "at a point where the river forked . . . in latitude 38° 46′ 47″ north." The trigonometrical survey was made on the return trip, connecting with Beechey's chart of ten years earlier, and the party returned to the ship on November 24. Belcher left for Monterey on November 30, but he revisited San Francisco briefly on September 21, 1839, while he was stopping at Bodega, and again a few days later in working down the coast. The high point on the Sacramento was probably the Feather River (situated at about 38° 47′ north latitude), but no chart of the river explorations was published, even one promised to Vallejo not having been delivered. Belcher was of course surprised not to find the three rivers emptying into Suisun Bay as shown on Beechey's chart; he personally saw only the Sacramento, having missed the mouth of the San Joaquin and, of course, the Jesús María.[75]

French interest in the American west coast was again expressed in 1837 and 1839, though San Francisco was apparently not one of its prime objectives. Abel Dupetit-Thouars anchored the *Vénus* at Monterey from October 18 to November 14, 1837. Looking out for French interests, particularly in the whale fisheries, he did not sail to San Francisco, but a party went up in Captain Hinckley's *Kamamalu* to obtain water and make observations, remaining from October 26 to November 1 and preparing a plan of the entrance and anchorage.[76] A round-the-world expedition headed by Cyrille Pierre Théodore Laplace in the frigate *Artémise* was at San Francisco four days beginning August 20, 1839. Anchoring below the presidio, Laplace visited the presidio and peninsula and "spent his short stay," according to Bancroft, "apparently in waiting to get away." His report, published after the gold rush, nevertheless expressed great admiration for the bay, particularly for the Yerba Buena anchorage.[77]

Another type of visitor was John A. Sutter, who landed from the *Clementine* at Yerba Buena on July 1, 1839. Securing at Monterey Governor Alvarado's permission to select a place of settlement inland, he sailed three small boats up the Sacramento River in mid-August, making what was almost a filibustering expedition into

California's northern interior. Exploring as far upstream as the Feather River, he at length fixed his choice upon a site near the junction of the Sacramento and its American fork, far removed from governmental authority. The establishment of Sutter's Fort was an important step in the development of San Francisco's hinterland, and New Helvetia very soon became the farthest outpost on the northern frontier and the first center of civilization at the end of the overland trail.[78]

One of the most comprehensive reports compiled by any of the early observers at San Francisco was drawn up by Eugène Duflot de Mofras, detailing a semi-official tour made by him in 1841. An attaché of the French legation at Mexico, he wished to discover what opportunities were offered to Frenchmen on the northwest coast. He sailed to Monterey on the *Ninfa* in May 1841, visited Sonoma, Ross, and San Francisco, and was again in Monterey early in July. Until October 18, when he embarked on the *Cowlitz* for Vancouver, he made his headquarters at Monterey and San Francisco, during which time he traveled to many points about the bay and in the interior, including a journey (probably by river) to Sutter's Fort in September. He returned from Vancouver to San Francisco on the *Cowlitz* with Sir George Simpson on December 30, 1841, but continued immediately to Monterey and San Blas. His published account includes a map, much information regarding the topography of the area, and a Frenchman's view of its civilization. Accompanying the description of the Sacramento is a summary of the available data pertaining to the long reputed Jesús María River.[79]

William D. Phelps, trading on the coast during the years 1840 to 1846, was at San Francisco Bay in the *Alert* in July 1841, and having been assured by his acquaintance, John A. Sutter, that no keel boat had ever navigated the Sacramento, he proposed to secure the honor of being the first to make that voyage. With six men in a cutter he left the ship on July 27 and arrived at Sutter's on the 29th. A week was spent in exploring above New Helvetia, after which he returned to the *Alert* in three days. Phelps may have sailed further upstream than any before him; he was the first American citizen to make the inland voyage.[80]

The first scientific exploring expedition from the United States to be sent into the Pacific reached the west coast in 1841. From the Columbia River, Commander Charles Wilkes dispatched two separate parties to California, one, under Lieutenant Cadwalader Ringgold, sailing in the sloop of war *Vincennes* to San Francisco, the other going overland. Leaving the north on August 7, 1841, the ship anchored off Yerba Buena on the 14th but was transferred three days later to Sausalito, where a year-round supply of water was available. On the 20th Ringgold with six boats set out to survey the Sacramento and on the 22nd reached Sutter's New Helvetia, which the party judged to be the all-season head of navigation. On the 26th they were at the Feather River junction, after which they passed the Sutter Buttes and on August 31 reached a point calculated to be in 39° 13′ 39″ north latitude. This, the northernmost point of the survey, was just beyond the present town of Colusa. Descending to Sutter's embarcadero by September 4, they terminated the survey at the mouth of the Sacramento on the 8th and boarded the *Vincennes* the next day. Meanwhile examinations had been made of San Pablo Bay and, between August 20 and 29, of the San Joaquin River. The land party under Lieutenant Emmons reached California late in September and made its way down the Sacramento Valley to Sutter's Fort, where it arrived on October 19. There a detachment embarked in one of the *Vincennes*' boats and proceeded to San Francisco by the 24th. The main body of Emmons' party continued cross country to Mission San Jose, rounded the bay, and arrived at Yerba Buena on October 28 by way of Santa Clara and Dolores missions. During the absence of the survey parties from the *Vincennes*, the remaining officers (including Wilkes) arrived at Sausalito in the *Porpoise* and the *Oregon* and made visits to several bay points: Martínez' ranch at Pinole, Captain Richardson's farm at Sausalito, the San Rafael mission, and Vallejo's Sonoma residence. Wilkes also went to Santa Clara mission and the pueblo of San Jose. The ships sailed on November 1, 1841, and, after Wilkes had spent an uncomfortable night's anchorage upon the San Francisco bar, shaped their course for Monterey.

Wilkes published a long, prejudiced, and, in many instances, inaccurate account of the San Francisco visit. He outdid both Duflot de Mofras and Simpson, the two other distinguished foreign visitors

of the same year, in expressing disapproval of the Mexican administration, and he viewed both the country and its people with a thoroughly jaundiced eye. His official map of the Sacramento River was
not published until 1858, after it had ceased to be of practical value,
but a privately published map incorporating the results was issued
by him in 1849.[81]

Following the French and American visitors came Sir George
Simpson in the *Cowlitz* on December 30, 1841. As a Hudson's Bay
Company representative he was engaged in a round-the-world tour
as official observer and commercial emissary. As inspector for the
company he was interested in the store which had been set up at
Yerba Buena the previous August, and his intercourse with the Californians was probably calculated as much to encourage their good
will as to obtain a view of the company's prospects. He spent January 5 with Vallejo at Sonoma, and then sailed for Monterey on
January 12. His narrative, published after the American conquest,
furnishes an interesting view of the bay and its commerce, but his
lively and often sarcastic comment was not well gauged to encourage the friendly relations he sought.[82]

One who styled himself "The King's Orphan" may well be considered California's first tourist. G. M. Waseurts af Sandels, a
worthy Swede educated at the king's expense and required in return
to visit a foreign land and prepare a journal of his observations,
arrived at Monterey from Acapulco in September 1842. With no
axe to grind, national, commercial or scientific, he visited San Jose
and Santa Clara, Yerba Buena, San Rafael, Petaluma, and Sonoma,
then returned to Yerba Buena and sailed to San Diego. He was soon
back at San Francisco and made a boat trip to New Helvetia, stopping en route in the region of Mt. Diablo. He continued upstream
beyond Sutter Buttes and returned to San Francisco by way of
Mission San Jose. Before departing for the Sandwich Islands, he
visited briefly at Bodega, then embarked at Yerba Buena. His journal, with its many careful observations and water color drawings,
merits more attention than it has received.[88]

John C. Frémont arrived at San Francisco in 1846, too late to
make important geographical explorations, but the last notable explorer before the American conquest. He had been in California in

1844 and recuperated at Sutter's Fort from March 10 to 22, but he did not go to the bay. He concluded at that time, and he was not the first to do so, that no river from the interior of America could penetrate the Sierra to San Francisco Bay. On his third expedition he made a second entry into California, reaching Sutter's Fort on December 9, 1845. After failing to meet the main body of his party in the San Joaquin Valley, he returned to New Helvetia and set out in Sutter's launch for Yerba Buena. On the way to inspect the silver mine at New Almaden, he sailed down the bay to Alviso, and later he journeyed to Monterey by way of the peninsula, soon becoming involved in the political and military affairs which wound up in the American conquest. Frémont's chief geographical contribution at San Francisco was to nomenclature, he having suggested the name Golden Gate which became permanently affixed to the bay's famous portal.[84]

The seizure of California by the United States in 1846 and the incidents of the Mexican War stimulated the movement of Americans into the country. Several years of well calculated American propaganda favorable to settlement in California had also begun to take effect when, in January 1848, the discovery of gold on the American Fork of the Sacramento River drew to California restless and fortune-hunting peoples from all over the world. Soon San Francisco Bay became the port of entry for a fantastic new commerce. The first steady traffic the bay had known coursed up its rivers or anchored before Yerba Buena. Sailing charts were in demand, and Cadwalader Ringgold, who had accompanied Wilkes in 1841 and was again at San Francisco in 1849, complied with the request of San Francisco citizens to prepare a series of charts for immediate issue. His surveys of the bay and the Sacramento River, the first under American rule, were derived from Beechey's observations of 1826 and his own investigations made in 1841 and 1849; they served the practical mariner well until superseded by the perpetually revised charts published by the United States government.[85]

THE MAPS OF
SAN FRANCISCO BAY

1769-1847

MAR DEL

MAR DEL SUR

CARTA REDUCIDA DEL
OCEANO ASIÁTICO,
Ó MAR DEL SUR,

QUE COMPREHENDE LA COSTA ORIENTAL Y OCCIDENTAL DE LA PENÍNSULA

DE LA CALIFORNIA, CON EL GOLFO DE SU DENOMINACION ANTIGUAMENTE CONOCIDO POR LA DE

MAR DE CORTÉS,

Y DE LAS COSTAS DE LA AMÉRICA SEPTENTRIONAL DESDE EL YSTHMO QUE DE DICHA

PENÍNSULA CON EL CONTINENTE HASTA EL RIO DE LOS REYES Y DESDE EL RIO COLORADO

HASTA EL CABO DE CORRIENTES.

Compuesta de orden del Ex.mo Señor Marqués de Croix, Virrey, Governador, y Capitan General
del Reyno de la Nueva España, y de los Exercitos de S. M.

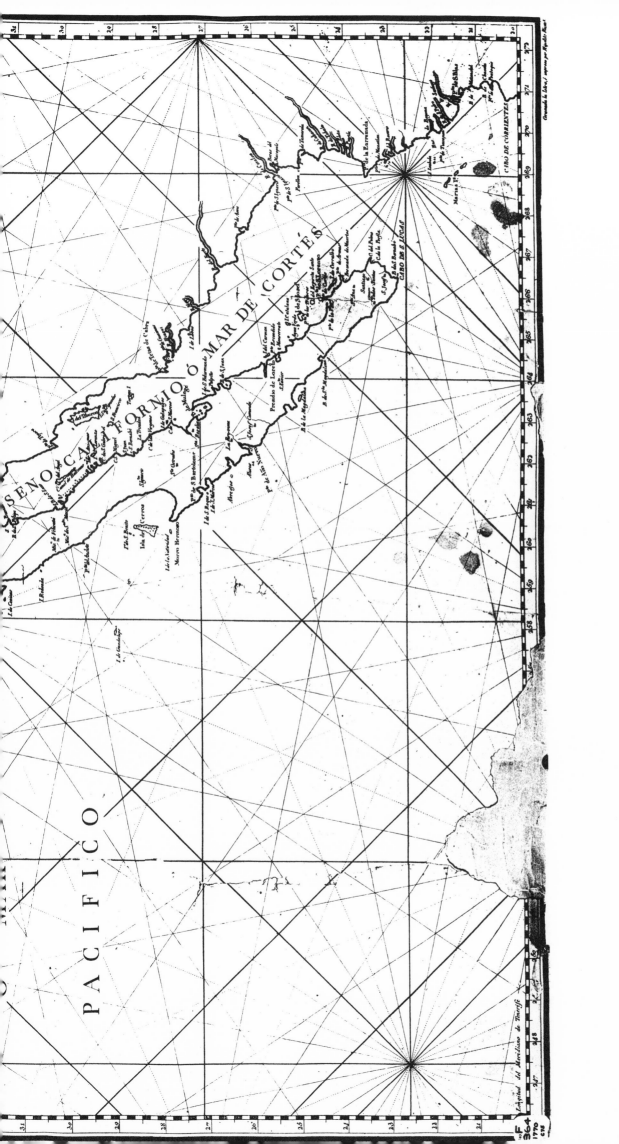

Carta reducida del Oceano Asiático, ó Mar del   1771
Súr, que comprehende la costa oriental y occi- Miguel Costansó
dental de la península de la California, con el
golfo de su denominacion antiguamente conocido por la de Mar de Cortés, y de las costas de
la América Septentrional desde el isthmo que
une dicha península con el continente hasta el
Rio de los Reyes, y desde el Rio Colorado hasta
el Cabo de Corrientes. Compuesta de orden del
Exmo. Señor Marqués de Croix, virrey, governador, y capitan general del reyno de la Nueva
España, y de los exercitos de S. M. . . . Mexico,
y octubre 30 de 1770. Miguel Costansó. (Madrid, Impreso por Hipolito Ricarte, 1771.)

72 x 82 cm.
In right lower margin: "Gravada la letra, é impreso por Hipolito
Ricarte." Left lower margin: "D. Tomás Lopez geógrafo de los
dominios de S. M. lo gravó en Madrid año de 1771."
"Longitud del meridiano de Tenerife."

※※※※

A CHART of the California coast, the first to show the bay of San Francisco,
discovered in 1769. Upon a similar manuscript chart of 1770, from which
this was derived, the bay did not appear, it having been added by Costansó
to the printed edition.

1771
Miguel Costansó

Miguel Costansó (fl. 1769-1811) was an army engineer who came to California as a member of the Portolá party of 1769, sailing to San Diego on the *San Carlos*. From there he made the first journey to San Francisco Bay and the next year was with the party which re-discovered Monterey and established a settlement there. On July 9, 1770, he left California with Portolá and Juan Pérez, arriving in Mexico City on August 10, where he, with Pérez, Vicente Villa, and Pedro Fages, was promoted for his part in the California expedition. In 1769 he was an *alférez* or ensign, but he attained the rank of *mariscal de campo* or major-general and became prominent in his profession. He had, in 1768, been a member of a *junta* called to deliberate on the project to occupy California and in 1769 and 1770 was one of the principals in carrying out the plan. In 1772 he reported favorably on the proposal by Juan Bautista de Anza to establish a land route between Sonora and California, thus contributing to the settlement of San Francisco, and in 1794 he prepared an *informe* regarding the fortifications of the California coast. He later assisted with plans to drain Mexico City through the Huehuetoca canal, with the construction of fortifications at Vera Cruz, and with other military projects.[1]

Costansó's *Carta reducida* was made, according to information contained in the title, at the order of the Viceroy, the Marqués de Croix, from diaries of the pilots of the 1769 and 1770 expeditions, fragments of manuscripts by missionaries and other explorers along the Pacific and Gulf coast, and from the personal observations of Costansó. In manuscript form, also dated October 30, 1770, it was appended to Costansó's official *Diario histórico*.[2] In this state it was probably finished or nearing completion before Costansó set out for California, for it does not show the new-found bay of San Francisco. Between October 1770 and the date of publication in 1771, Costansó apparently made a revision, adding the "Estero de S. Francisco" and making other minor changes. The new map, still bearing the 1770 date in the title, was engraved in Madrid by Tomás López, geographer, and printed there by Hipólito Ricarte in 1771. Although San Francisco Bay is but a small detail, it is strikingly well drawn, its general outline being more true in shape and better oriented than it is in the chart produced by the official survey of 1775. The bay is probably based upon sketches made by Costansó in 1769; he records the making of a rough map of the outer Bay of the Farallones,[3] Pedro Fages mentioned this or another map by Costansó,[4] and it is not unlikely that other preliminary sketches were prepared.

Copies: Bancroft Library. Thomas W. Streeter. Archivo General de Indias (103-3-23 and 104-3-4).

Reproductions: Academy of Pacific coast history, *Publications*, 1909-1919, v. 2, no. 4, frontispiece. Palóu, *Historical memoirs*, 1926, v. 2, p. 48.

Listed: Wagner, No. 625. Lowery, *Descriptive list*, No. 539. Torres Lanzas, No. 255.

Additional notes: Of the manuscript of 1770, not showing San Francisco Bay, a copy is in the British Museum (Add. manuscript, 16752b), and another is in the archives of the Ministerio de Guerra, Madrid (J 9a 22 ea). A printed reproduction is found in Watson, *Spanish occupation of California*, 1934, frontispiece. Photostat in Pomona College Library.

This map of 1770 was published in London by Alexander Dalrymple in 1790 as the *Chart of California, by Miguel Costansó, 1770. Engraved by Tomás Lopez, Madrid, 1771,* (followed by the original title in Spanish). Dalrymple's chart was not a facsimile of the 1770 manuscript but a redrawing, apparently engraved, to add to *An historical journal* (a translation of Costansó's diary) issued in 1790. The chart is occasionally found separately in the collections of charts made by Dalrymple. A copy is found in the Dalrymple collection in the Library of Congress (v. 3), and one is in the Pomona College Library. It is listed as Wagner, No. 747, and Phillips, *List of geographical atlases,* No. 543 (p. 281).

1771
Miguel Costansó

1772
Juan Crespí

Mapa de lo substancial del famoso Puerto y Rio de San Francisco explorado por tierra en el mes de marzo del presente año de 1772, sacado por el diario y observaciones del R. P. Fr. Juan Crespí, missionero apostolico del colegio de propaganda fide de franciscos observantes de San Fernando de Mexico, y ministro de la nueva mission de Monterrey. Se omiten los arroyos corrientes, y dulces, arboledas, y rancherias de gentiles por la precision, y ser mapa abierto. Todo desde la punta del estero (donde desagua un buen rio) para adelante abunda mucho mas: Y los gentiles desde la bahia arriba se hallaron rubios, blancos, y barbados. Y todos muy buenos, y afables que regalaron a los Españoles con sus frutas y comidas.

45 x 63 cm. Manuscript.

"Escala de 20 leguas Españolas a 17 y ½ cado grado."

CRESPÍ's is the first separate map of San Francisco Bay of which we have knowledge and includes the entire bay from the ocean to the interior rivers. It is a curious bit of cartography both because of the ingenuous and picturesque manner in which it is made and the distorted impression of the

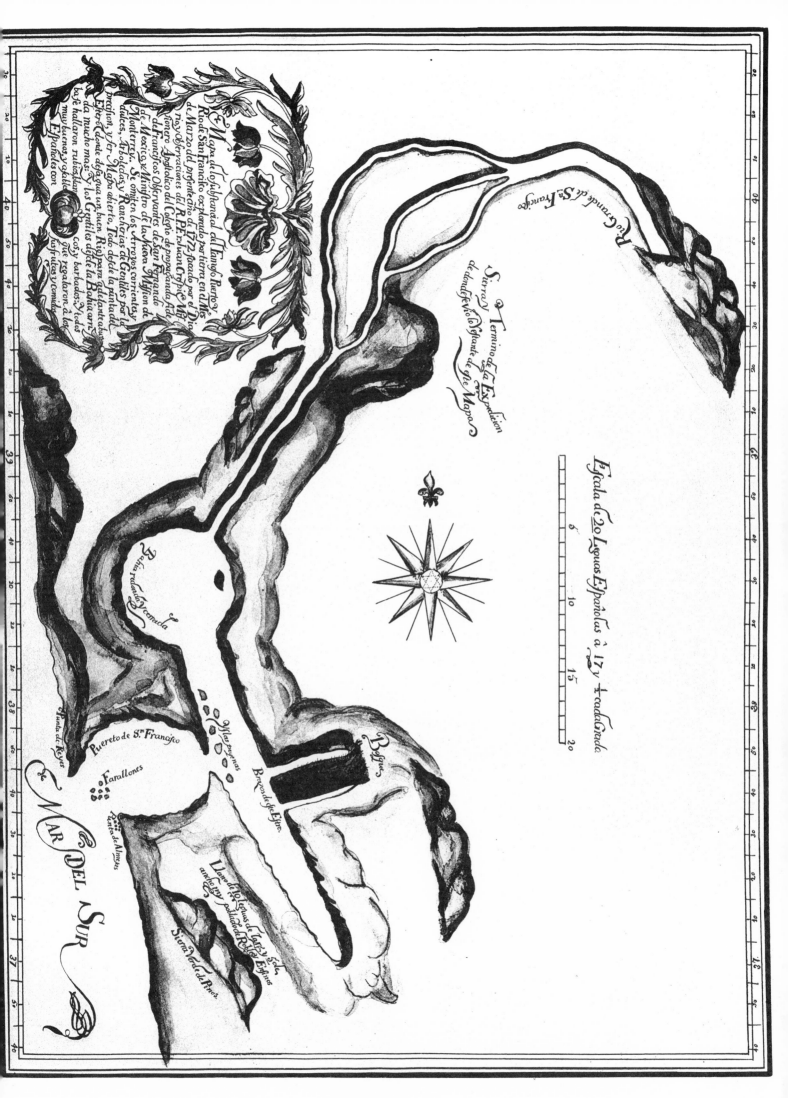

Map No. 2

topography which it presents. Nevertheless, it depicts the salient features of the region as described by its author.

Fray Juan Crespí (1721–1782) was a native of Mallorca and came to America with his friends Palóu and Serra in 1749. Previous to his emigration from Mexico to California he served as a missionary to the Apaches of Sierra Gorda. After the expulsion of the Jesuits in 1767 he was transferred to the California peninsula, where he was put in charge of Mission Purísima Concepción. In 1769 he accompanied Portolá as a member of the first land party to reach Upper California, and from San Diego he, like Costansó, made the journey to San Francisco and return. He went to Monterey in 1770 and assisted Serra in founding Carmel mission, which place became his home for the next twelve years. In 1772 Crespí accompanied Pedro Fages on his expedition up the east bay shore through the present Alameda and Contra Costa counties when the rivers which entered San Francisco Bay on the northeast were discovered, and in 1774 he made a last long voyage with Juan Pérez to Alaska. He died at Carmel in 1782. Crespí was a consummate diarist, and his records give an intimate, somewhat naive, but exceedingly detailed picture of the lands and peoples which he visited.[1]

The *Mapa* of 1772 was made by Crespí to accompany his diary of the Fages expedition of that year to San Francisco Bay, and references to work on the map during the journey are found in his account. The map is as significant as it is odd, for it graphically records the prevailing confusion regarding the area. The outer Bay of the Farallones is compressed into a shape comparable to the existing Golden Gate Channel, with the seven Farallones guarding its entrance. Along the northern shore of this open bay appears the name "Puerto de Sn. Francisco," identifying the old San Francisco Bay situated near Point Reyes. Tributary to old San Francisco is the new and unnamed bay, comprising the "two great estuaries" of which Crespí wrote, one terminating in the south, the other leading to the lake-like "Bahia redonda" (San Pablo) and the far "River of San Francisco." The map is a picturesque compromise between Crespí's first-hand observations and the traditional topography of the region.

Two examples of the manuscript are found, with varying titles. That in the Archivo General de Indias, Seville, is quoted above. The other in the archives of the Ministerio de Guerra, Madrid, bears the following legend: *Carta del Puerto y Río de Sn. Francisco explorado por tierra en el mes de Marzo del presente año de 1772, formado por el diario del R. P. Fr. Juan*

[33]

1772

Juan Crespí

Crespey, *misionero apco. del Colegio de Franciscos, observantes de propaganda fide de S. Fernando de Mexico y ministro de la na. mision de Monterrei.*[2] Crespí's original diary and map were given to Palóu,[3] who sent them to the Franciscan college of San Fernando in Mexico. Fr. Rafael Verger, guardian of the college, then apparently had a copy of them made which he sent to Spain, this map being the one now in the Archivo General.[4] Although Wagner attributes the copy to Verger,[5] the map is certainly Crespí's, the copying, perhaps, Verger's. Whether the *Carta del Puerto* in Madrid is the original, also transported to Spain, or yet another copy is not known. Other contemporary copies were made.[6]

Copies: Archivo General de Indias, 104-6-14. Ministerio de la Guerra, Archivo de mapas, L. M. 8a.-1a.-No. 41 (varying title; measuring 60½ x 46 cms.) [Dr. Herbert E. Bolton has a hand drawn facsimile in his possession.]

Reproductions: Palóu, *Historical memoirs*, 1926, v. 2, p. 344. Bolton, *Anza's California expeditions*, 1930, v. 1, p. 400. Wagner, *Spanish southwest* (special illustrated ed.), 1924, p. 268. *Sierra club bulletin*, v. 13, p. 56, Feb. 1928. (All are from the copy in the Archivo General.)

Listed: Wagner, No. 628. Lowery, *Descriptive list*, No. 557 (varying title).

⇶⇶⇶[3]⇷⇷⇷

plano del puerto de San Francisco, registrado   1775
por el paquebot de S. M. San Carlos, al mando   José de Cañizares
del Theniente de Fragata de la Real Armada
Don Juan Manuel de Ayala, en este año de 1775.

75 x 71 cm. Colored manuscript.

"Los sitios que tienen la señal de un ancl[a] son fondeaderos resguardados."

"Hallase este puerto situado en la latitud norte 37° 53 ms. Longitud
occidental del meridiano del Puerto de San Blas 17° 10 ms."

"Es copia del original remitido al excmo. señor virrey de estos rey-
nos, que saque de orden de S. E. Mexico 30 de noviembre de 1775.
[Signed] Diego Panes."

27 features are identified by a table on the face of the chart.

⇶⇷

THIS CHART is a product of the first regular survey of San Francisco Bay,
made in August, September, and October 1775. The expedition to San
Francisco was ordered by the viceroy to precede and make preparations
for the arrival of colonists to be led overland from Mexico by Juan Bautista
de Anza; Juan Manuel de Ayala was in command.

José de Cañizares came to California in 1769 in the first land expedition
to San Diego, captained by Rivera y Moncada. Though a *pilotín*, or pilot's
mate, he was sent with the land party to take observations and prepare a
diary. He remained at San Diego during Portolá's first journey to San
Francisco and was not present at the founding of Monterey. In 1773 he was
adjudged too young to rank as a commander of a transport vessel, but by
March 1774 he had become master of the *San Antonio*, perhaps because of
lack of older competent navigators. After accompanying Ayala to San
Francisco in 1775 and making the first entry through the Golden Gate,
he returned to San Blas, going to San Francisco again the next year as master
of the *San Carlos* and assisting in the erection of the presidio and in making

[35]

1775
José de Cañizares

the renewed explorations of the bay. He was a member of the Arteaga expedition to the northwest coast in 1779 and for many years thereafter was captain of one of the California transports. He was at Monterey in 1784 at the time of Serra's death and as late as 1790 was in California in command of the *Aranzazu*. Cañizares made the first actual survey of San Francisco Bay, assisted by Aguirre, the work having been assigned to him by Ayala. He prepared the official report and drew the first chart based upon a regular survey, making a revised chart the next year to include the new findings. Cañizares was highly recommended by Ayala to the viceroy as an able and honest officer, exhibiting great talent in his profession and being worthy of advancement.[1]

Cañizares' chart of 1775 includes within its limits the outer Bay of the Farallones, flanked by its seven islands, and the modern bay of San Francisco extending as far inland as Suisun and the mouths of the tributary rivers. It is significant for its omissions as well as for its content; although the chart bears the title *Plano del puerto de San Francisco*, it does not show the old bay of San Francisco with which the great inner bay had always been associated. The map of 1775 may be said to mark the advent of San Francisco Bay as a cartographic entity.

The chart was constructed from information obtained by Cañizares and his men during extensive explorations of the bay in the ship's boat. Data secured with sounding line and compass were blended with personal observations and impressions, and the result was not precise in orientation or proportion. As in Crespí's map, the Bay of the Farallones is too constricted from north to south. San Francisco Bay proper (the southern arm) is far too short and bears too much eastward, while the size of Hunter's Point is greatly exaggerated. Present day Mare Island, Island No. 1, and Tubbs Island are lumped into a single land mass in the north end of San Pablo Bay, and the creeks, sloughs, and river are not noted. It is interesting to find that modern Yerba Buena or Goat Island was named Isla de Alcatraces in the survey while present day Alcatraz Island remained unnamed. Soundings are shown and, on the land, the location of a number of redwood groves is indicated.

Cañizares drew the chart while the expedition was still in San Francisco Bay, to accompany the official report which he signed "in this new port of San Francisco, at the shelter of Angel Island, on September 7th, 1775."[2] These documents, which went with Ayala's report dated at San Blas, No-

[36]

vember 9, 1775, were sent to the viceroy,[3] who forwarded copies to Spain including a copy of the map, signed by Diego Panes and bearing the date November 30, 1775.

Copies: Archivo General de Indias, Carpeta de mapas, 6 (bearing a note that it is a copy; presumably the original remained in Mexico).

Reproductions: Palóu, *Historical memoirs*, 1926, v. 4, p. 40. Bolton, *Anza's California expeditions*, 1930, v. 1, p. 385.[4] Eldredge, *March of Portolá*, 1909, p. 64. Richman, *California under Spain and Mexico*, 1911, chart V, p. 110. Masters, *Historical review of the San Francisco exchange*, 1927, p. 7. Photostat in Pomona College Library.

Listed: Wagner, No. 640. Lowery, *Descriptive list*, No. 569. Torres Lanzas, No. 305.

1775
José de Cañizares

⟫⟫⟫[4]⟪⟪⟪

1776 Plano del puerto de San Francisco.

José de Cañizares

44½ x 33½ cm. Manuscript.

46 features are identified by a table on the face of the map.

⟫⟫⟪⟪

THE CHART shows the results of the reëxamination of the bay and the exploration of the river delta in 1776 at the time of the founding of the presidio and mission of San Francisco.

[For biographical data about Cañizares, see No. 3.]

After the departure of Juan Bautista de Anza from California early in May 1776—he had brought colonists overland for San Francisco—Governor Rivera y Moncada sent expeditions to make establishments at San Francisco Bay, and the presidio and mission were dedicated in September and October. While supplies were being unloaded from the *San Carlos*, an examination of the upper bay and rivers was undertaken. Gabriel Moraga, with a land party of soldiers, and Fernando de Quirós, Cañizares, and Father Cambón in the ship's boat agreed to join forces within three days at Carquinez Strait to undertake a combined exploration of the rivers. They failed to meet at the rendezvous, however, and as Moraga had most of the provisions, the boat party was forced to return while the soldiers made a quick march of four days up the Sacramento River and into the plains. As shown by the map, some additional observations were made among the islands in the delta beyond Suisun Bay before the boat began the return trip. Before going back to the presidio, Quirós and his party rowed up Petaluma Creek and ascertained that it did not connect with Bodega Bay, settling a question which had been raised by Bodega y Quadra the previous year. According to Palóu, Cañizares claimed upon his return that he had seen nothing which had not been examined the previous year, "that the map which he made of that first exploration was very accurate, and that he had nothing to take away or to add";[1] this statement is belied by Cañizares' own map of 1776.

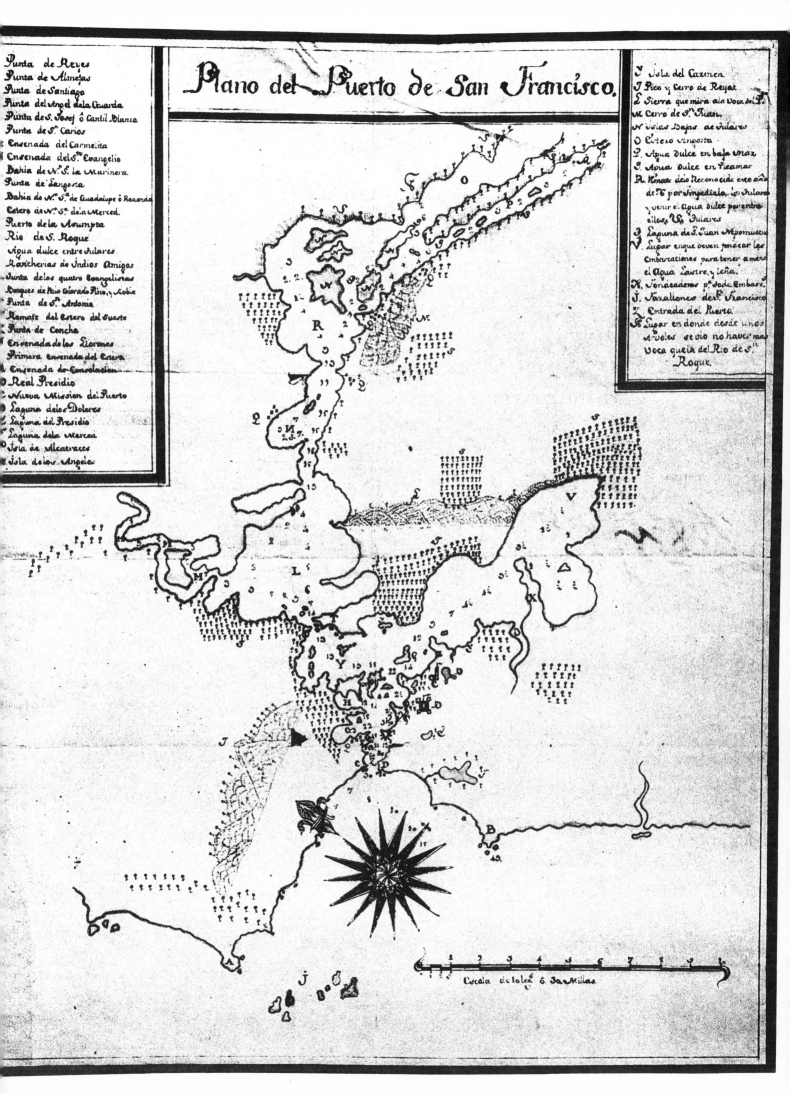

Plano del Puerto de San Francisco.

Map No. 4

The *Plano* is undated, but Wagner cites a note to the map to prove it was made in 1776.[2] Certainly the new information dates from that year. The chart is clearly a revision of the one of 1775, though not a tracing of it. The chief innovations are, as expected, in the regions of the river delta and the northern shore of San Pablo Bay. What is now known as Petaluma Creek has been added, and Mare Island Strait (the mouth of the undiscovered Napa River) has been identified. The locations of the new presidio and mission are shown, and a number of place names have been added. A redrawing of essentially the same chart was published in 1781.[3]

Copies: Ministerio de Guerra, Madrid, 9a 2a a 27.

Reproductions: California historical society quarterly, v. 14, p. 111, June 1935. Photostat in Pomona College Library.

Listed: Wagner, No. 653.

1776
José de Cañizares

1776 Plan de la boca del Puerto de San Francisco,
Pedro Font situado en 37°. 49´.

26 ½ x 18 cm. Manuscript.

A MAP of the entrance to San Francisco Bay made in March 1776 during the Anza expedition to San Francisco. It was sketched from the elevated cliff at Fort Point.

Father Pedro Font, a Catalan, was in 1775 at the Franciscan mission of San José de Pimas in the Mexican state of Sonora. He was a man of liberal education and a mathematical turn of mind, and was sufficiently celebrated to have been chosen as one competent to take the observations required during Anza's second overland expedition to California. He accepted the viceroy's appointment to this position and traveled from Sonora to California, went to explore and select sites for the presidio and mission at San Francisco, and returned to Mexico. Serving not only as "navigator," he also kept a detailed diary, observed and recorded latitudes and distances, made maps, said masses, exhorted his people, and preached to the Indians. If he proved to be querulous, pessimistic, irritable, and narrow in his moral and religious views, he was also painstaking, enthusiastic, and imaginative and was entirely equal to the assignment he had accepted. His maps and diaries showed him to have a sharp eye, a sensitive nature, and a faculty for graphic and artistic expression.[1]

Father Font, in company with Juan Bautista de Anza, Gabriel Moraga, and a party of soldiers, went up the San Francisco peninsula from Monterey in March 1776 and arrived at Fort Point on the 27th. Here he sketched the mouth of the port, continuing his observations with the aid of the graphometer through the 28th.[2] The resulting map is not to be harshly criticized, considering that it was drawn largely from observations made from a single point; but, for this reason perhaps, the perspective is not true, the shape of the land being considerably elongated in a northwest-southeast direction. Topographic features are suggested, and the route of the expedition is marked. The drawing of a ship at the southwestern tip of Angel Island represents the place of anchorage of the *San Carlos* in the previous autumn.[3] Font placed two crosses on the map, the one at Point Lobos showing the site of the wooden cross which was set up by Rivera in 1774 and the other at Fort Point representing the one raised by Anza and Font.[4] The Mexican league in which the map is calibrated is equivalent, according to Bolton,[5] to about 2.6 miles.

The apparatus used by Font to make his computations included a poor compass secured from the mission of San Xavier del Bac, a fine astronomical quadrant furnished by the viceroy and an astrolabe and graphometer obtained at Mission Carmel in California. His latitudes were calculated by tables compiled in 1756–1759 by Jorge Juan, based on the meridian of Cádiz, and consequently required two corrections. The computations were not often exact, as Font himself observed, and his errors were not consistent, but the latitude which he recorded for San Francisco was but two minutes in error.

Font inserted the map in the diary at the end of the entry for March 28. As it is mentioned in both the long and short diaries, it may be that two copies were made by him. The short diary (now in the Bancroft Library) is without maps at the present time. It was compiled in Ures, Mexico, after Font had returned from the California expedition. Later he went to the mission of Tubutama, where he leisurely wrote the complete diary (now found in the John Carter Brown Library), to which this map and three others were appended. Whether the short diary originally included maps is not known.[6]

Copies: John Carter Brown Library (accompanying Font's complete diary).

Reproductions: Brown University, *San Francisco and California in 1776*, 1911 (last map). Bolton, *Anza's California expeditions*, 1930, v. 4, p. 342. Eldredge, *Beginnings of San Francisco*, 1912, v. 1, p. 132.

Listed: Not found.

≫≫≫≫≫[6]≪≪≪≪≪≪≪

1776 [Map of the east bay shore, east-southeast of the Pedro Font mouth of the port.]

7 x 11 ½ cm. Manuscript.

A MAP showing two arms of the bay (San Antonio and San Leandro creeks) and the "Grove of trees which is east-southeast of the mouth of the port" (on the Alameda peninsula); drawn on April 1, 1776, during the Anza expedition to San Francisco Bay.

[For biographical data regarding Font, see No. 5.]

After exploring the San Francisco peninsula, Anza's party went south to the site of Palo Alto, circled the lower end of the bay and proceeded northward along the foothills, thus avoiding the swampy land adjoining the bay. On the first day of April, when somewhat beyond the site of present day Mills College, the men ascended a hill, and from this eminence Font made a small map of the Alameda peninsula below.[1] The expedition then continued the journey toward San Pablo Bay.

The map includes the east bay mainland from north of San Antonio Creek (now the Oakland estuary and harbor) to San Leandro Creek. The intervening grove was situated on the Alameda peninsula (now an island) and represented part of the virgin stand of trees which was to give Oakland its name. The mouth of the bay and the adjacent tips of San Francisco and Marin peninsulas are shown. The four islands are probably Angel Island, Alcatraz, Yerba Buena, and Brooks Island.

The map is included in the text of the complete diary,[2] and no mention of it is made in the short diary.

Copies: John Carter Brown Library (in Font's complete diary).

Reproductions: Brown University, *San Francisco Bay and California in 1776*, 1911, p. 6. Bolton, *Anza's California expeditions*, 1930, v. 4, p. 362. Richman, *California under Spain and Mexico*, 1911, p. 111.

Listed: Not listed.

39 ... **39**

Sierra Nevada.

TULARES.

Campo verde.

La Goleta Sonora.

Punta de Reyes.

I

o 99

o 100

a

b

c

101

Valle de Sta Fulgino.

Valle de Sta Coleta.

38 ... **38**

H

Punta de Almejas.

o 95

98

Bosque

R. de la Harina.

102

d

o e

95

94 96
de S. Matheo.

97

Rio de Guadalupe.

103

R. de S. Franco.

93

Llano de los Robles.

R. de S. Cupertino.

92

Ojo 4

R. de las Llagas.

Valle de Sn Bernardino.

MAR DEL SUR.

37 ... **37**

Punta de Año nuevo.

Rio del Paxaro.
Valle de Sn Pasqual.

La 91
Natividad

Valle de Sta Delfina.

5   10   15

Escala de quinze leguas Mexicanas.

Punta de Pinos.

105
Rio de Monterey.

Monterey.
106
M. Carmelo.

P. F. Petrus Font fecit. Tubutama. anno 1777.

PLAN, O MAPA DEL VIAGE QUE HICIMOS DESDE MONTEREY AL PUERTO DE Sn FRANCISCO.

⟫⟫⟫⟫⟫[7]⟪⟪⟪⟪⟪⟪

Plan, o mapa del viage que hicimos desde Mon- 1777
terey al Puerto de Sn. Francisco.   Pedro Font

38½ x 26 cm. Manuscript.

"P. F. Petrus Font fecit. Tubutama anno 1777."

MAP OF the Anza expedition of 1776 from Monterey to San Francisco, drawn by Font at Mission Tubutama, Mexico, after his return from California.

[For biographical data regarding Font, see No. 5.]

Font drew four maps of the expedition: one of the mouth of the bay, another of the portion of the east bay shore (these two done in California), a general map of the entire route of the expedition from Mexico to San Francisco and return, and this, which is virtually an enlargement of the Monterey-to-San Francisco section of the general map.[1] Like the others, this shows the route of the expedition and the numbered camp sites, and it suggests the general topography of the country, including the "Tulares" and a bit of the Sierra Nevada beyond California's great interior valley. The letters "H" and "I" placed near the Golden Gate and Carquinez Strait refer both to the diary and to a table lettered upon the general map. The schooner *Sonora* is depicted at the entrance of Bodega Bay, referring to the voyage of Bodega y Quadra there in 1775, and the undetermined limits of Tomales Bay in the direction of San Francisco point to the contemporary question raised by Bodega whether the two bays were joined.[2] Font's contention that the rivers entering Suisun Bay to the north were no rivers at all but "much water in a pond"[3] is likewise expressed in his map, which shows the tributaries as an extension of the bay itself into the Tulares. The general impression of the bay is good; though less detailed than the survey by Cañizares in 1775 and 1776, the general proportions are somewhat better. Point Richmond is shown as an island.[4]

1777
Pedro Font

Font records the making of at least four copies of the map: the first on April 10, 1776; the second for Father Serra on the 11th; and the third for Anza on the 12th, all done at Carmel mission, where Font was recuperating from his journey. Because Font says on the 12th that a fourth copy was made and enclosed with the diary, it would seem that perhaps a fifth was drawn and dated at Tubutama mission in 1777 (the one here quoted); however, Font's long diary was composed at Tubutama in 1777, and it is likely that this statement was inserted at that time.[5] The map is not mentioned in the short diary.

Copies: John Carter Brown Library (with Font's complete diary). Archivo General de Indias, 104-6-18. British Museum, Add. ms. 17,651 (16) (with title in upper left hand corner).

Reproductions: Brown University, *San Francisco Bay and California in 1776*, 1911 (next to last map). Bolton, *Anza's California expeditions*, 1930, v. 4, p. 302. Eldredge, *Beginnings of San Francisco*, 1912, v. 1, p. 140.

Listed: Wagner, No. 655. Lowery, *Descriptive list*, No. 587.

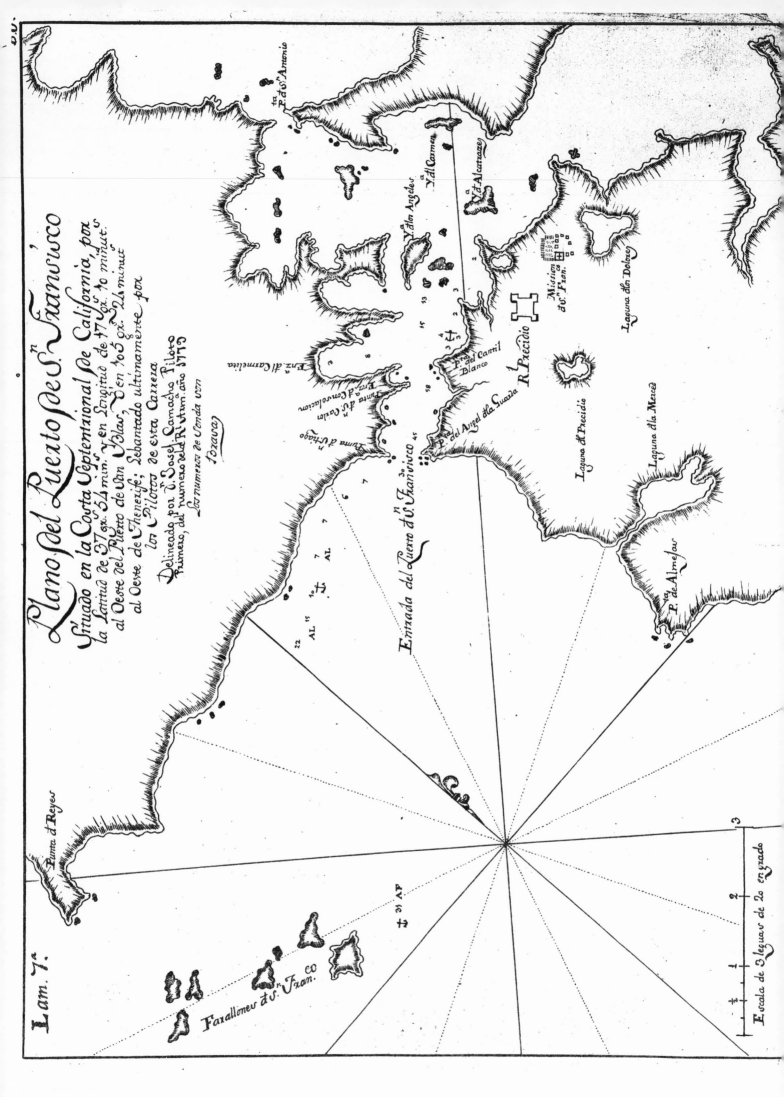

Lam. 7ª

Plano del Puerto de Sⁿ Francisco

Situado en la Costa Septentrional de California, por la Latitud de 37 gr. 51 min. y en longitud de 47 gr. 40 minutᵒˢ al Oeste del Puerto de San Blas, y en 105 gr. 26 minutᵒˢ al Oeste de Thenerife; Levantado ultimamente por los Pilotos de esta Carrera

Delineado por Dⁿ Josef Camacho Piloto Primero, del numero de la Rᵗ Armᵃ año de 1779

Los numeros de Sonda son Braras

Punta de Reyes

Pᵗᵃ de Sⁿ Antonio

Yª del Carmen
Pᵗᵃ de Alcatrazes

Yª de los Angeles

Misiⁿ de Sⁿ Fran.ᶜᵃ

Laguna de Dolores

Enzᵃ del Carmelita

Pⁿ del Carril Blanco

R. Precidio

Punta de Catlo
Enzᵃ de Convalecion

Laguna del Precidio

Laguna de la Merced

Punta de Santiago

Pⁿ del Angel de la Guarda

Entrada del Puerto de Sⁿ Francisco

Pᵗᵃ de Almejar

Farallones de Sⁿ Fran.ᶜᵒ

Escala de 3 leguas de 20 en grado

Map No. 8

>>>>>>>[8]<<<<<<<

plano del puerto de Sn. Francisco, situado en   1779
la costa septentrional de California, por la latitud   Josef Camacho
de 37 grs. 54 mins. y en longitud de 17 grs. 10   y Brenes
minuts. al oeste del puerto de San Blas, ó en
105 grs. 24 minuts. al oeste de Thenerife; le-
bantado ultimamente por los pilotos de esta carrera. Delineado por Dn. Josef Camacho, piloto
primero, del numero de la rl. arma., año 1779.

27 ½ x 37 ½ cm. Manuscript.

"Los numeros de sonda son brasas."

THE CHART shows the results of the reëxamination of the port in September and October 1779 by members of the Arteaga expedition on the return voyage from Alaska.

Camacho was a regular member of the Spanish naval force at San Blas, where he served from about 1779 to 1790 both as pilot and commander on voyages to the northwest coast. During the Arteaga-Bodega expedition to the far north in 1779 to widen the Spanish knowledge of that remote sector of their Pacific world, Camacho was first pilot of the *Princesa* and prepared maps and a diary of the voyage. In 1787 he was in charge of the San Blas naval establishment and was ordered to take command of the *Concepción* and, with Mourelle in the *Favorita*, to determine the extent of Russian encroachment at Nootka. Illness, perhaps due to old age, in November 1787 prevented him from accepting the assignment, and Martínez y Zayas was appointed in his place. Wagner considers him to have been too old to take part in the 1789 expedition to fortify Nootka.[1] In addition to this 1779

1779
Josef Camacho y Brenes

chart of San Francisco Bay, Camacho also made the official chart of the Arteaga expedition, one of the California coast which included San Francisco, dated 1785, another of the Pacific, and perhaps a *Plano del puerto de Santiago* of 1779.[2]

While returning from the northwest coast in 1779, the *Princesa* and *Favorita* became separated during a calm and both proceeded to San Francisco, although they had not previously intended to touch there. Arteaga arrived on the 14th, Bodega on the 15th of September, and the time until their departure on October 30 was spent in working on the diaries and charts of the explorations and in re-surveying the port of San Francisco, which had not been examined since 1775–1776.[3] The resulting chart depicts only that part of the bay contiguous to the tips of the Marin, San Francisco, and Point Richmond peninsulas, from Point Reyes and the Farallones southward to Hunter's Point. On a larger scale and including a smaller area than the Cañizares charts of 1775 and 1776, after which it was apparently patterned, it shows but little improvement over the earlier models. The influence which it exerted over later maps may be traced by noting the position of Lake Merced, which differs in the Camacho and Cañizares surveys.

Copies: Library of Congress.

Reproductions: Pacific historical review, v. 16, p. 368, Nov. 1947. Photostat in Pomona College Library.

Listed: Wagner, No. 667.

Plan del gran Puerto de San Francisco des-   1781
cubierto y demarcado por el Alferez Graduado   José de Cañizares
de Fragata de la real armada, Dn. Jose de Cañi-
zares primer piloto del Departamento de San
Blas. Situado en la costa occidental de la California al norte de la linea en el Mar Asiatico en
atitud norte 37 gs. 44. minutos, y gravado por
Manuel Villavicencio Añ. de 1781. [México?
1781.]

17 X 12 cm.

31 features are identified by a table of symbols on the face of the
map.

⇝⇝⟨⟨⟨

THE FIRST printing of Cañizares' chart of the bay, probably the first separate published map of San Francisco Bay.

[For biographical data about Cañizares, see No. 3.]

The chart was copied largely from the 1776 Cañizares *Plano*, but a few
of the features (e.g., the Punto de año nuebo) are from the chart of 1775.
It was probably printed in Mexico.[1]

Copies: In 1934 a copy was in the possession of Douglas Watson, San
Francisco, and another belonged to G. R. G. Conway, Mexico (both found
in copies of Palóu, *Relación histórica de la vida ... del venerable padre Fray
Junípero Serra*, 1787).

Reproductions: California historical society quarterly, v. 13, p. 181,
June 1934. Davis, *Seventy-five years in California*, 1929, p. 6. Photostat in
Pomona College Library.

Listed: Wagner, No. 678.

**1785
Josef Camacho
y Brenes**

𝔈ste pedaso de costa de la 𝕮alifornia está leban-
tado por los pilotos de esta carrera, y enmendado
ultimamente en el año de 1785 por el 𝔄lferz. de
𝔑avio y 𝔓rimer 𝔓iloto 𝔇n. 𝔍oseph 𝕮amacho y
𝔅renes.

35 x 44 cm. Manuscript.

"Longitudes al oeste del meridiano de San Blas."

➤➤➤◀◀◀

A CHART of the coast from Point Arguello to Bodega Bay, including the
bay of San Francisco. Because the detail of San Francisco Bay is an expansion of the Camacho chart of 1779, it is included in this study.

[For biographical data about Camacho, see No. 8.]

From hydrographic and descriptive notes collected at the Spanish naval
establishment at San Blas, charts of the northwest coast or of significant
parts of it were prepared for the use of the pilots. This is one of the compiled maps, as indicated in the title, its final revision having been made in
1785 by Camacho. San Francisco data may be traced to the Cañizares chart
of 1776 and Camacho's survey of 1779; the delineation of the bay as expressed here followed closely the standard Spanish chart of San Francisco
Bay which was to appear in print several times during the next forty years.[1]

The chart has pencil emendations of a later date, showing the location of
coastal missions.

Copies: Sociedad mexicana de geografía y estadística, México.

Reproductions: Photostat in Pomona College.

Listed: Wagner, No. 704.

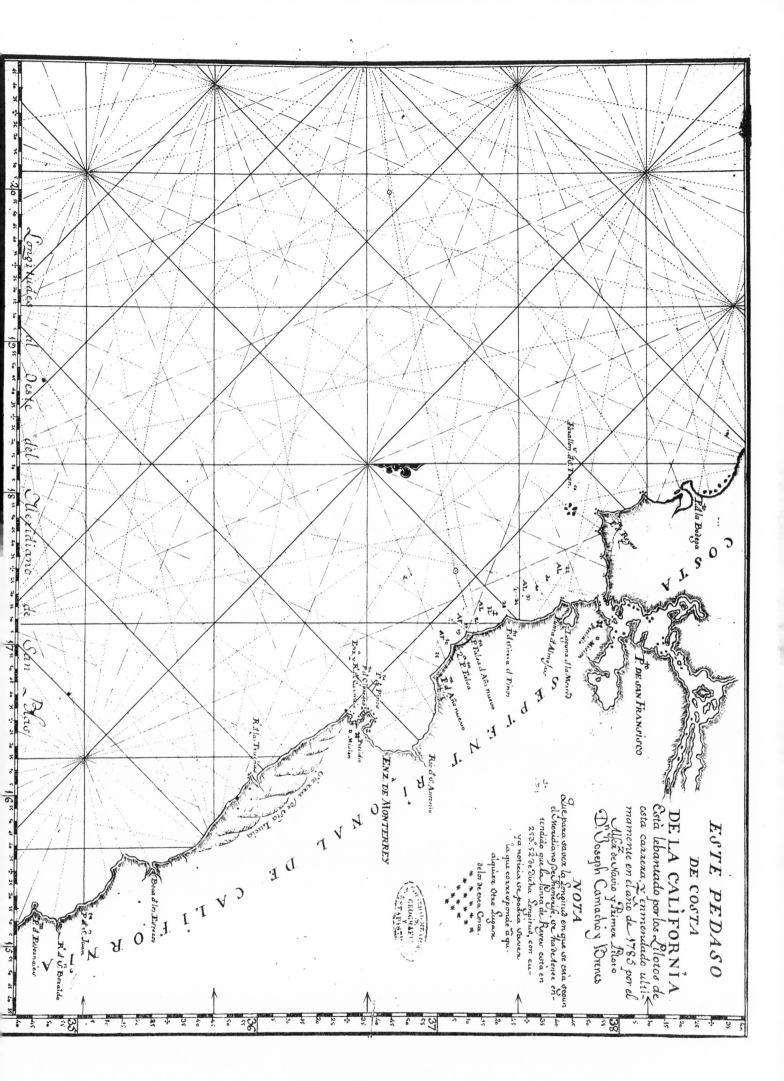

ESTE PEDASO
DE COSTA
DE LA CALIFORNÌA

Map No. 10

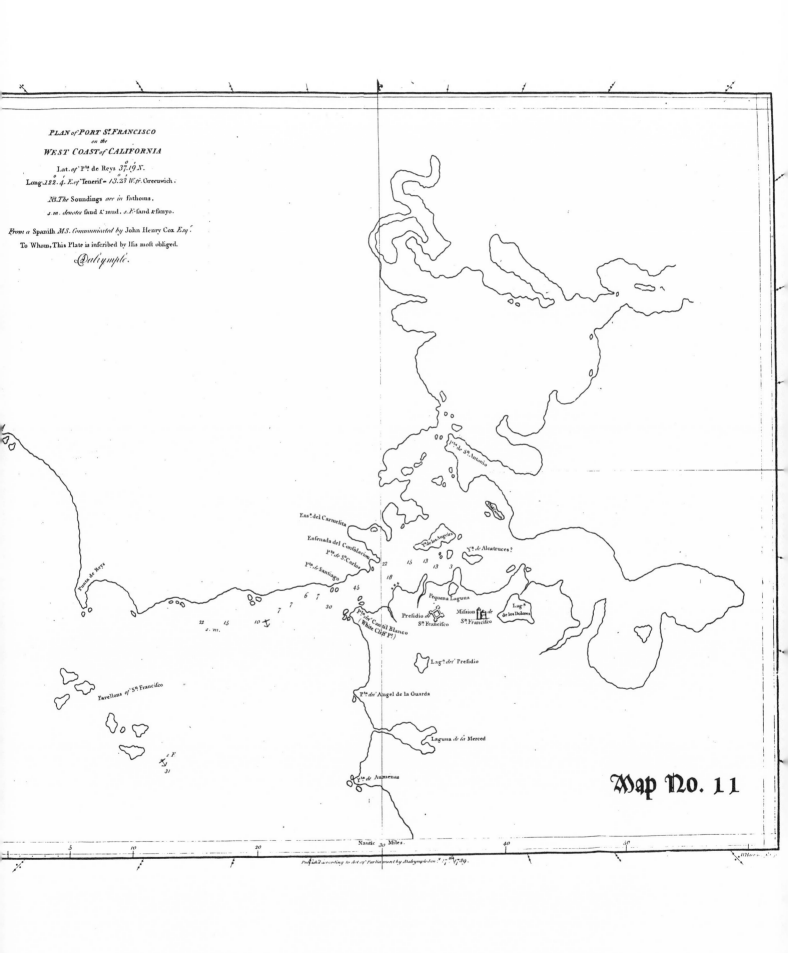

PLAN of PORT St. FRANCISCO
on the
WEST COAST of CALIFORNIA

Lat. of Pta de Reys 37.19 N.
Long. 122.4. E. of Tenerif = 13.23 W. fr. Greenwich.

N.B. The Soundings are in fathoms.
s. m. denotes sand & mud. s. F. sand & fanyo.

From a Spanish M.S. Communicated by John Henry Cox Esqr.
To Whom, This Plate is inscribed by His most obliged.
Dalrymple.

Pta de Sn Antonio

Ensda del Carmelita

Enfenada del Confalacion
Pta de Sn Carlos

Pta de Santiago

Pta de los Angeles

Yta de Alcatruces ?

22
15 13 13 3
18
45

Punta de Reys

22 15 10
s. m.

7 7 6 7 30

Pequena Laguna

Presidio de   Mision de
Sn Francisco   Sn Francisco

Lag.a de los Dolores

Pta del Can El Blanco
(White Cliff Pt.)

Lag.a del Prefidio

Farellons of Sn Francisco

Pta del Angel de la Guarda

s F
31

Laguna de la Merced

Map No. 11

Pta de Aumenas

Nautic 30 Miles.

5   10   20   30   40   50

Publish'd according to Act of Parliament by Dalrymple Jan.r 1st 1789.

11

Plan of Port Sn. Francisco on the west coast of California . . . from a Spanish MS. communicated by John Henry Cox, Esq. to whom this plate is inscribed by his most obliged Dalrymple.

1789

Alexander Dalrymple

29½ x 33½ cm.

"Lat. of Pta. de Reys 37°. 19′ N. Long. 122°. 4′ E. of Tenerif—13°. 23′ W. fr. Greenwich. NR. The soundings are in fathoms. s.m. denotes sand & mud. s.f. sand & fanyo."

At bottom: "Published according to act of Parliament by A. Dalrymple, Jany. 17th, 1789."

At bottom, right: "W. Harrison, sculp."

⇒⇒⇐⇐

AN ENGRAVED chart of San Francisco Bay derived from Spanish sources. Published in England, it is the earliest known map of the bay in the English language.

Alexander Dalrymple, first hydrographer to the British Admiralty, veteran employee of the East India Company, voluminous author and publisher, brought out for the English public a number of charts and texts relating to the northwest coast of America. From Spanish sources he obtained two charts of San Francisco Bay, several of the coast line and its separate harbors, and a translation of Costansó's account of the 1769 expedition, all of which were published by him. These he supplemented with English-made charts of the region.[1]

The 1789 *Plan* was the first public appearance of an important Spanish chart of San Francisco Bay. The original "Spanish MS." from which it was taken is apparently not now known, but it probably dated from about 1785 and may have been compiled by Camacho. Judging by the appearance of

1789 Alexander Dalrymple

the Dalrymple edition and of later and perhaps more exact copies, the manuscript chart had its origin in the Cañizares *Plano* of 1776 and Camacho's observations made at San Francisco in 1779 (see his *Plano del puerto* of that year). The supposed chart closely resembled the San Francisco Bay detail of Camacho's *Pedaso de la costa de la California* of 1785, but certain data, for example the soundings outside the Golden Gate, indicate that the earlier chart of 1779 and its sources were also consulted. John Henry Cox, who sent the manuscript to Dalrymple, forwarded to him at about the same time a *Plan of the Inlet of Bucareli . . . discovered in 1775 . . . and minutely examined in the expedition of 1779.*[2] As both of these charts were published by Dalrymple in 1789, and they also appeared together in the LaPérouse atlas of 1797, this association suggests their common origin in the 1779 expedition. It is likely, however, that the "Spanish MS." was compiled several years later from various sources, for it is in some respects less accurate than Camacho's *Plano* of 1779.

How or where John Henry Cox secured the manuscript is not divulged. Wagner believed the chart of Bucareli Inlet to have been obtained indirectly from Mourelle. Cox was an English resident of Canton in the late 1780s, from which place he engaged in the fur trade on the northwest coast. He was an associate of Captains James Hanna and John Meares, knew Captain George Dixon and other fur traders, and received charts of the coast from several of them. Cox's name was applied to a number of topographical features in the far north between 1786 and 1791, and two charts of portions of the island of "Oonalaska," issued by Dalrymple in 1791, were credited to Cox himself, though he may have been only an intermediary in their publication.[3] The manuscript chart of San Francisco Bay or a copy of it was probably current in Europe in 1797, for it was reproduced in the atlas of the LaPérouse *Voyage* issued that year. The 1789 chart was sometimes bound with the *Historical journal* by Costansó, published by Dalrymple in 1790.[4]

Copies: Library of Congress, Dalrymple collection [Charts and plans], v. 2, no. 47. Huntington Library, Dalrymple collection, v. 3, no. 87; and in Dalrymple's edition of Costansó's *Historical journal,* 1790.

Reproductions: Pacific historical review, v. 16, p. 369, Nov. 1947.

Listed: Wagner, No. 720. Phillips, *Geographical atlases,* No. 543 (v. 2, no. 47).

[50]

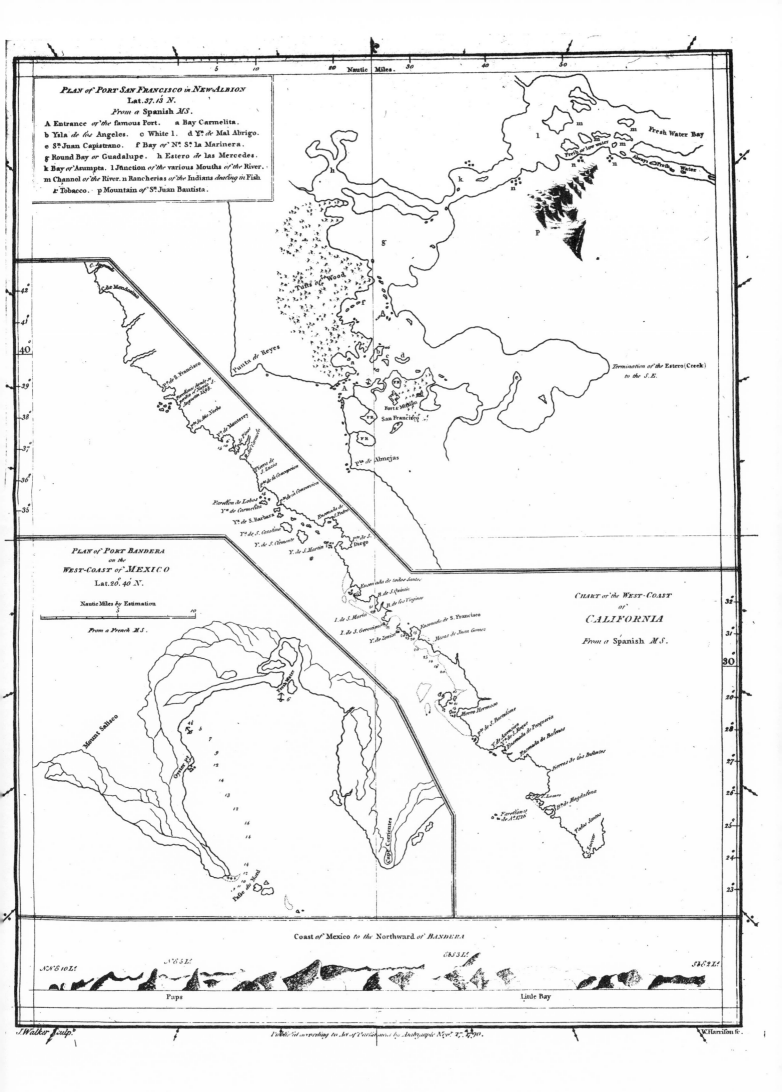

Map No. 12

12

Plan of Port San Francisco in New Albion... From a Spanish Ms. [London, 1790.]

1790
Alexander Dalrymple

Printed with two other maps on a sheet measuring 32 ½ x 24 cm.

"Lat. 37° 13′ N."

At bottom of sheet: "Published according to act of Parliament by A. Dalrymple, Nov. 27th 1790."

➤➤➤⟨⟨⟨

ONE OF three maps on a single sheet, issued by Alexander Dalrymple to be inserted in his edition of Costansó's *Historical journal*, published in 1790.[1]

If the chart was a true copy, the "Spanish Ms." was a curious source, and its identity is not known. Differing from the chart of the bay published by Dalrymple in 1789, it is a strange mixture of ingredients derived from the charts of 1775 (the large island in San Pablo Bay), 1776 (Suisun Bay and the river channels), and other unidentified or imaginary origins. It is doubtless a compiled map and is less accurate than the San Francisco chart issued by Dalrymple the previous year. Thirteen features are identified by letters on the face of the map.

Copies: Found in copies of Costansó's *Historical journal*, 1790, in the Henry E. Huntington and John Carter Brown libraries.

Reproductions: Winsor, *Narrative and critical history of America*, 1889, v. 8, p. 212. Davidson, *Identification of Sir Francis Drake's anchorage*, 1890 (next to last map; an incomplete tracing).

Listed: Wagner, No. 748.

1792
George
Vancouver

Entrance of Port Sn. Francisco.

21 x 26 cm.

"Latde. 37°. 48′. 30″. N. Longde. 237° [!]. 52′. 30″. E. Varn. 15°. 00′ E."

⟼⟼⟩⟨⟵⟵

A CHART of the entrance to San Francisco Bay prepared by the English expedition under George Vancouver.

Vancouver, a companion of Captain James Cook on his famous voyages, returned to the Pacific to continue the examination of the northwest coast so well begun by Cook for the English nation. He was particularly instructed to look for the northwest passage and investigate sections of the coast which had been neglected by his predecessors. He was also to meet at Nootka with representatives of the Spanish government to discuss a settlement of the territorial dispute then current between the two countries. Though coöperative surveys were carried out in northern waters, the negotiations relating to the Nootka Sound controversy came to naught, and Vancouver continued his southward voyage along the coast. He reached San Francisco Bay on November 14, 1792, and the *Discovery* was the first foreign vessel to enter the bay. Permitted great freedom by the local authorities in making his observations, he nevertheless was satisfied with the Dalrymple chart which he apparently carried with him[1] and was content only to chart for himself the immediate entrance of the port, showing the usual places of anchorage. Vancouver sailed from the bay on November 25, 1792, but returned the following year, remaining from October 19 to 24, 1793. That time his movements were greatly restricted by an anxious governor, and in 1794 he passed the harbor by, stopping only for a short time at Monterey.[2]

The chart represents but cursory observations made at the harbor entrance, showing Vancouver's route of approach and departure, the Golden Gate Channel, and Angel and Yerba Buena islands. Except for the designation of the presidio, no place names were used, a directional nomenclature having been adopted for a few landmarks. The anchorages are at Richardson's Bay, below the Spanish fort, and in Yerba Buena Cove. The latter anchorage was supposed by Bancroft to have been at North Beach, but a comparison of the relative positions of Yerba Buena Island and the place of anchorage shown on Vancouver's chart with the chart published by Dalrymple in 1790 (and carried by Vancouver) seems to prove that its location was at Yerba Buena Cove.[3]

Copies: In the atlas to Vancouver, *A voyage of discovery to the north Pacific Ocean and round the world,* 1798 (inset to plate 8). It also appears with French text as the *Entrée du port Sn. Francisco* in the *Atlas du voyage* accompanying the French edition of Vancouver's *Voyage,* 1799.

Reproductions: Eldredge, *Beginnings of San Francisco,* 1912, v. 2, p. 498 (English edition of chart).

Listed: Wagner, No. 856.

1792
George
Vancouver

14

1794
José Joaquín
de Arrillaga

Plano que manifiesta el Puerto de San Francisco cituado en la costa septemtrional de Californias en 37° 48´ de altura de polo N y en 17°
33´ al Ote. del meridiano de San Blas como hace
mismo el fuerte nombrado de San Joaquin colo-
cado en la Punta del Cantil del mismo puerto
construido por el Señor Governador interino
de la Peninsula de Californias, D. Jose Joaquin
de Arrillaga en el presente año de 1794 por orden de Exmo. Señor Conde de Revilla Gigedo
virrey de N. E. advirtiendose que los lienzos de
muralla qe. lleve el color de carmin indica ser de
cal y canto y lo restante que hace frente a la entrada del puerto es de peña viva.

61 ½ x 92 cm. Colored manuscript.
"Nota que desde la superficio del agua en la Punta del Cantil esta
el canto alto de la muralla tiene de elevacion 120 pies."

≫≫≫≪≪≪

Two PLANS on a single sheet, one of the *Puerto de S. Francisco*, showing
the entrance to the bay, the other of the *Punta del Cantil* (Fort Point) upon
which appears a diagram of the Castillo de San Joaquin, or fort, erected in
1794.

As *ad interim* governor of Alta California from 1792 to 1794, Arrillaga
shared with officials in Mexico the general alarm aroused by the increased

operations of the English along the coast. The commercial rivalry between Spain and England which had come to a head in the Nootka affair of 1789 was brought to the attention of the Californians by the receipt of a warning from Mexico aimed particularly at British vessels along the coast. Among other precautions taken against the English, of which a proposed settlement at Bodega in 1793 was one, was the viceroy's plan to strengthen the California presidios. Arrillaga reported on the system of defenses in July 1793, the Castillo de San Joaquin at the Punta del Cantil was completed in December, and the map of 1794 was doubtless prepared to show the conditions at San Francisco. The plan did not reach Mexico until 1795, it having been forwarded there by the succeeding governor, Diego de Borica.[1]

The chart of the *Puerto de S. Francisco* shows the mouth of the bay and is designed to give the position of the fort and show the ship lane. The innermost point is the Pta. de la Yerba Buena, opposite what is erroneously labeled the Ya. de Los Angeles (modern Yerba Buena Island). The name Ya. de Alcatraces, which probably belonged to Yerba Buena Island at that time, is here attached to the island now so called. Eleven place names appear on the face of the map in addition to the labels belonging to the fort and presidio.

Copies: Archivo general, Mexico (Californias, v. 47, no. 8).

Reproductions: Richman, *California under Spain and Mexico*, 1911, p. 344. Photostat in Pomona College library.

Listed: Wagner, Nos. 826, 827. Phillips, *California*, No. 188. Bolton, *Guide*, p. 160-161.

Additional notes: Several additional plans of the defenses at Fort Point and of the presidio have been noted:

The original plan of the presidio executed by José de Cañizares in 1776 (see Palóu, *Historical memoirs*, 1926, v. 4, p. 124) has apparently not been preserved.

On March 4, 1792, Hermenegildo Sal sent the governor a description of the presidio, *Informe sobre los edificios de San Francisco*, accompanied by a plan. A copy of the original documents appears in *California archives, Provincial state papers*, v. 11, p. 50 (Bancroft Library, Cal. Ms. A-6). The diagram was published (redrawn) in Bancroft, *California*, 1886–1890, v. 1, p. 695.

An undated plan of the *Castillo de San Joaquín* at Fort Point is included in the Alviso *Documentos para la historia de California*, p. 156. Bancroft

1794
José Joaquín de Arrillaga

1794
José Joaquín de Arrillaga

presumed the diagram to have been prepared about 1794, but it differs considerably from Arrillaga's plan of the same year. It is reproduced (redrawn) in Bancroft, *California*, 1886–1890, v. 1, p. 699.

A map of the *Presidio de San Francisco, 1820*, secured by Edward Vischer from M. G. Vallejo, has also been preserved. It shows the structure as a square, indicates the character of the surrounding terrain and orients the plan in relation to the Castillo and to Mission Dolores. The original is in the Bancroft Library; a reproduction, copied from a tracing made by George Davidson, is found in Eldredge, *Beginnings of San Francisco*, 1912, v. 2, p. 722.

15

Plan du port de St. Francois, situé sur la côte de la Californie septentrionale. La Pointe des Rois par 37°. 59′. de latitude nord et 124°. 54′. de longitude occidentale. [Paris, 1797.]

1797 Jean Francois Galaup de LaPérouse

47 x 32 ½ cm.

"L. Aubert, scripsit."

"Les sondes sont exprimées en brasses d'Espagne, de deux vares ou six pieds de Castille."

"Lieues marines de 20 au dégré."

A key to 21 identifying symbols appears on the face of the map.

A chart of Spanish origin reproduced in the atlas to the *Voyage* of La-Pérouse, 1797.

LaPérouse, while pursuing his round-the-world voyage in the French interest, sailed southward along the California coast in 1786, passed San Francisco Bay on September 10, and arrived at Monterey on the 13th. He remained there until the 24th, then set out for the Philippines, on the next leg of his ill-fated voyage. Preceding Vancouver by six years, LaPérouse was the first foreigner to bring a vessel into a California port, and he was received with great hospitality. California seemed to offer little advantage to French commerce, and the expedition did not touch at San Francisco or at other California ports,[1] although charts of San Francisco and San Diego, as well as of Monterey, were introduced into the published atlas of the voyage.

The Monterey chart was made under LaPérouse's orders while the *Boussole* and *Astrolabe* were anchored in that port, and several Spanish charts, perhaps one of San Francisco Bay, were later secured by LaPérouse at Manila from the pilot Mourelle.[2] LaPérouse was on good terms with the San Blas naval officers who were at Monterey during his stay there, and some hydrographic material may have been secured from them. It may be,

1797
Jean François
Galaup de
LaPérouse

however, that the chart of San Francisco Bay was obtained by the editors of the *Voyage* from European sources. It was derived from the same original as the Dalrymple *Plan* of 1789, and it is almost identical with (and may have been the source of) the *Plano del puerto* published by the Mexican government in 1825. Its cartographic antecedents were the Cañizares chart of 1776 and the charts of 1779 and 1785 by Camacho.[8] Although LaPérouse paid his visit to California in 1786, the San Francisco chart was not a product of the expedition, and it has therefore been catalogued under 1797, the date of its publication. Several charts of the coast in the atlas include San Francisco Bay as a detail, particularly plates 16 and 31; these were apparently derived from the Camacho chart of 1785, and they vary in several respects from the accompanying large scale map of the bay.

Copies: In LaPérouse, *Atlas du voyage,* 1797, plate 33. Also issued in English as the *Plan of Port St. Francisco in California* in the London edition of the *Voyage,* 1798, plate 33 (34½ x 22½ cm.).

Reproductions: Not found.

Listed: Wagner, No. 846. Phillips, *California,* No. 185.

16

Plan del Puerto d. Sn. Franco. situado en la costa de la California septentrional en la latitud N. de 37° 53′ y en longd. de ° segun el meridiano dl. Cavo Sn. Lucas, sondeado y demarcado con la maior exsactitud por los oficiales y pilotos dl. Departamento de Sn. Blas.

1803
Departamento
de San Blas,
México

75 x 53 cm. Colored manuscript.

➤➤❳❮❮

A MAP compiled from hydrographic data available at the royal naval station at San Blas.

The exact date and sources of this map are not known. It is both better and worse than a chart of the bay ought to have been at the end of the 18th century. The coast line of the outside Bay of the Farallones resembles the chart of 1775; the southern arm of the bay is like the 1777 chart of Font; San Pablo Bay is reminiscent of Crespí's "Bahia redonda y cerrada;" and the "Desembocadura d. los ríos de Sn. Franco.," beyond the Strait of Carquinez, is not a very discriminating representation of Suisun Bay and the river mouths. Place names were derived chiefly from the surveys and diaries of 1775 and 1776. Modern Yerba Buena Island, properly known as Los Alcatraces prior to 1826, is called El Deshabrigo (the place without shelter), a name which in the variant form of Ya. del Mal Abrigo appeared on the Spanish chart published by Dalrymple in 1790 (Cañizares had marked its inhospitable shores in 1775). The chart was compiled from various and conflicting materials on file at San Blas, emended, quite possibly, by the personal observations of the navigator-cartographers.

Wagner assigns the map tentatively to the year 1790, noting that in the Archivo General de Indias it is considered to belong probably to 1803.[1] There is nothing on the face of the map to settle the matter, but the later

1803

Departamento de San Blas, México

date has been chosen here, for in spite of the chart's inconsistencies, its general effect is modern.

Copies: Archivo General de Indias, Carpeta de Mapas, No. 9.

Reproductions: Richman, *California under Spain and Mexico*, 1911, chart VII, p. 112. Photostat in Pomona College library.

Listed: Wagner, No. 770. Torres Lanzas, No. 487. Phillips, *California*, No. 184 (dated 1776).

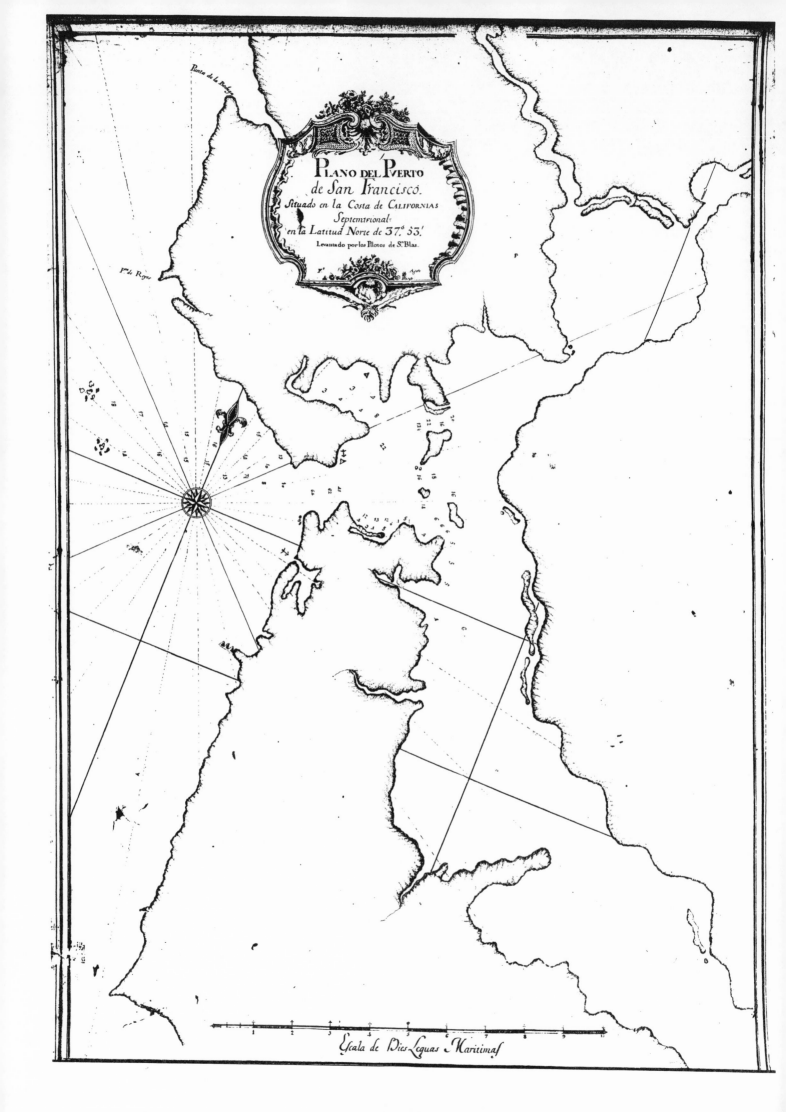

PLANO DEL PUERTO
de San Francisco.
Situado en la Costa de CALIFORNIAS
Septemtrional:
en la Latitud Norte de 37.° 53.'
Levantado por los Pilotos de S.ᵗ Blas.

Ponta de la Barra

P.ᵗᵃ de Reyes

Escala de Diez Leguas Maritimas

𝔓lano del 𝔓uerto de 𝔖an 𝔉rancisco. 𝔖ituado en la costa de Californias septemtrional en la latitud norte de 37°. 53'. 𝔏evantado por los pilotos de 𝔖n. 𝔅las.

1803
𝔇epartamento de 𝔖an 𝔅las, 𝔐éxico

66½ x 46 cm. Manuscript.
Beneath title appears: "Fr. Agote."
Scale in maritime leagues.

A CHART of the bay compiled from hydrographic data available at the Spanish naval station at San Blas.

This chart is similar to the one catalogued immediately above, but it is not identical in outline or appearance. Almost no attempt has been made to show relief, and only two place names have been used (Punta de la Bodega and Pta. de Reyes). Although somewhat smaller in size than the other map, it is on an appreciably larger scale. Neither map was made directly from the other, and both are unlike other maps of the bay which have been observed. Whether "Fr. Agote" was draughtsman or copyist is unknown.

Copies: Pomona College library.
Reproductions: Not found.
Listed: Wagner, No. 769.

1825
Comisión
Hidrográfica,
México

𝔓lano del 𝔓uerto de 𝔖an 𝔉rancisco, situado en la costa de la 𝔈alifornia septentrional, siendo la latitud de la 𝔓unta de los 𝔘eyes de 37°. 59'. norte, y su longitud 116°. 20'. ocidental del meridiano de 𝔈adiz. 𝔐éxico, año de 1825.

48½ x 33 cm.
"La sonda expresa brazas de dos varas Castellanas."
"Leguas marinas de 20 en grado."
An "Explicación" or key to 21 identifying symbols appears on the face of the map.

≫≫)≪≪

A REPUBLICATION under official Mexican auspices of the "Spanish MS." which was first brought out by Alexander Dalrymple in 1789 and reissued in 1797 in a different form in the atlas to the *Voyage* of LaPérouse. Except for the language and placement of the text, the computation of longitude from Cádiz, and the Mexican imprint, the 1825 edition was almost an exact reproduction of the chart of 1797.

The original manuscript chart from which this derives was made about 1785, probably by Josef Camacho. It obviously owed much to Camacho's *Plano del puerto* of 1779 and his *Pedaso de la costa de la California* of 1785, and it was consequently in debt to José de Cañizares' bay chart of 1776. Dalrymple obtained the manuscript from John Henry Cox, an Englishman who lived in China and participated in the northwest coast trade. The French editors of the LaPérouse *Voyage* may have copied the same original, and either the Mexican printing of it in 1825 followed the French, or both French and Mexican were faithful reproductions of the same source.[1] The chart of 1825 was printed and issued in separate form and was of course forty years outmoded on the day of publication.

Copies: Bancroft Library. Library of Congress.
Reproductions: None found.
Listed: Phillips, *California*, No. 190.

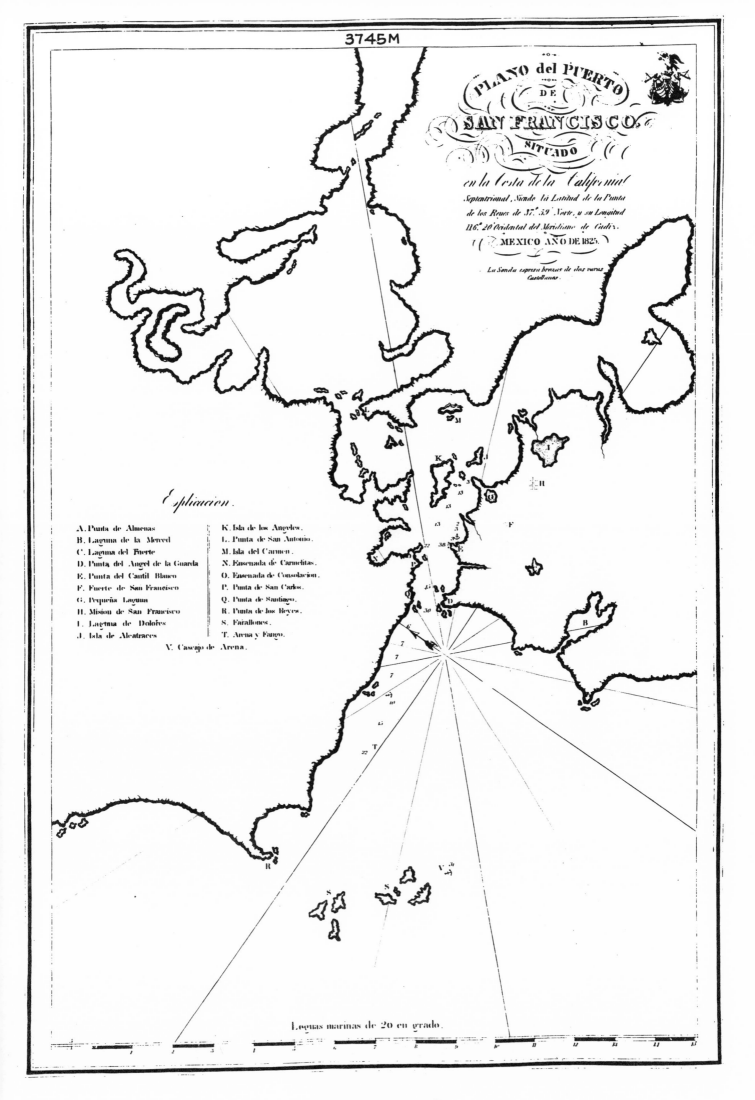

PLANO del PUERTO DE SAN FRANCISCO SITUADO

en la Costa de la California Septentrional, Siendo la Latitud de la Punta de los Reyes de 37.° 59' Norte, y su Longitud 116.° 20' Ocidental del Meridiano de Cadiz.

MEXICO AÑO DE 1825.

La Sonda espresa brazas de dos varas Castellanas.

Esplicacion.

A. Punta de Almenas
B. Laguna de la Merced
C. Laguna del Fuerte
D. Punta del Angel de la Guarda
E. Punta del Cantil Blanco
F. Fuerte de San Francisco
G. Pequeña Laguna
H. Mision de San Francisco
I. Laguna de Dolores
J. Isla de Alcatraces

K. Isla de los Angeles
L. Punta de San Antonio
M. Isla del Carmen
N. Ensenada de Carmelitas
O. Ensenada de Consolacion
P. Punta de San Carlos
Q. Punta de Santiago
R. Punta de los Reyes
S. Farallones
T. Arena y Fango

V. Cascajo de Arena

Leguas marinas de 20 en grado.

Map No. 18

Plan of the Harbour of San Francisco, New Al-   1827·1828
ion, by Captn. F. W. Beechey, R. N. F. R. S.   Frederick William
Assisted by Lieutt. Edwd. Belcher, Mr. Thos.   Beechey
Elson, master, and Mr. Jas. Wolfe, mate. 1827,
⟨2⟩8.

4½ x 58 cm. Manuscript.
Latitude of the fort, 37°. 48'. 30". N. Longitude [of the fort],
22°. 27'. 23". W. Variation 15°. 30'. E. Dip 62°. 35',2 N.
.Water, F & C. 9h. 42m. Rise 6 feet 0 in., at Yerba Buena."
⟨sc⟩ale in nautic miles.
⟨in⟩sets: elevation views of Table Hill (Mt. Tamalpais) and entrance
⟨of⟩ the bay; marks for locating Blossom Rock; and view of the Faral-
⟨o⟩nes from the hills of San Francisco.

⟫⟫⟩⟨⟪⟪

CHART of a wholly new survey of San Francisco Bay, made by members
the English expedition under Frederick William Beechey, R.N.
Beechey in the sloop *Blossom* came down from Bering Sea to San Fran-
⟨ci⟩sco in the fall of 1826. Having spent an unsuccessful season in the far
⟨no⟩rth prepared to succor the polar expeditions of captains Parry and Frank-
⟨li⟩n should they complete the perilous transcontinental passage, he dropped
⟨do⟩wn the coast at the closing in of the Arctic winter. Anchoring in San
⟨Fr⟩ancisco Bay on November 6, 1826, he remained there until December
⟨28⟩, then proceeded to the Sandwich Islands. After another fruitless sojourn
⟨in⟩ the Arctic the next year, the expedition reëntered San Francisco Bay on
⟨D⟩ecember 17, 1827, and on January 3, 1828, set out on the long homeward
⟨vo⟩yage to England. Beechey had been instructed before undertaking the
⟨ex⟩pedition to make careful surveys in the Pacific where such had not been
⟨pr⟩eviously completed, and his men were constantly engaged in this busi-
⟨ne⟩ss at San Francisco during the 1826 visit. Under Beechey's direction they

1827-1828
Frederick William Beechey

examined in two months' time the portions of the harbor which he felt wer[e] most likely to be frequented by vessels for some years to come.[1]

The survey embraced the whole bay as far inland as Carquinez Strai[t] and the resulting chart was a vast improvement over any which had pre[-] ceded it. It erred in one respect, taking at its face value a report that thre[e] rivers debouched into the far end of Carquinez Strait.[2] Beechey applie[d] the name Yerba Buena to the island now so known, and he transferred i[ts] former label, Los Alcatraces, to present-day Alcatraz Island. Blossom Roc[k] was named after his vessel. Mount Diablo (Sierra Bolbones), the east ba[y] redwoods, and several routes of travel were also laid down on the map The expedition was well received by the newly established Mexican regim[e] and was allowed great freedom of movement. In return Beechey agree[d] to supply the California governor with a copy of the San Francisco char[t]

Beechey's chart of the bay was drawn, at least in preliminary form, be[-] fore he left San Francisco in January 1828, for at that time he left the cop[y] with Commandante Ignacio Martínez. Governor Echeandía ordered it ser[t] to him at San Diego, which was presumably done, although Bancroft di[d] not discover it in the California archives, and it is not cited in guides to th[e] archives of Mexico and Spain. A curious coincidence has placed copies [of] Beechey's chart among records preserved in the town of Martinez, count[y] seat of modern Contra Costa County, California, site of Ignacio Martíne[z] Rancho Pinole. It has been supposed that these may have been copies of th[e] chart left by Beechey with Martínez in 1828, but as they are obviousl[y] similar to the published edition of 1833, it is likely that they are of a lat[e] date.[3]

Following the publication of the Beechey chart in 1833, it became th[e] authoritative guide to the bay and remained so until well into the America[n] period. Like the earlier charts by Cañizares and Camacho, it became th[e] source of a long line of copies and adaptations, a number of which are note[d] below.

Copies: The original manuscript chart of the bay is in the Hydrographi[c] Department, Admiralty, Bath, England. The copy reproduced here is fro[m] a photograph secured through the courtesy of K. St. B. Collins, Com[-] mander, R.N., Superintendent of Charts.

Reproductions: Not found.

Listed: Not found.

Additional notes: The earliest publication of Beechey's chart of the ba[y] apparently occurred in 1833. It was issued by the British Hydrographical Office as Hydrographical chart No. 591, and it included as an inset an enlarged detail of the entrance to the harbor. (See below, maps Nos. 20, 21.)

A section of the general chart of the bay, with additional geological data, appeared as the *Geological plan of the Port of San Francisco, California,* in *The geology of Beechey's voyage,* by J. Richardson, 1839. (See map No. 22.)

A similar portion of the map was also used as an inset to the map, *The coasts of Guatemala and Mexico . . . with the principal harbours of California,* published in Alexander Forbes' *California: a history,* 1839. (Map No. 23.)

Eugène Duflot de Mofras based his manuscript *Carte détaillée* of 1841 on Beechey's work, as well as the printed *Port de San Francisco* and *Entrée du Port de San Francisco* which were introduced into the atlas accompanying his widely circulated *Exploration* of 1844. (See maps Nos. 26, 28, 29.)

Charles Wilkes, whose U. S. Exploring Expedition was at San Francisco in 1841, adapted Beechey's configuration of the bay to augment his own survey of San Pablo Bay and the Sacramento River. The product was not officially published until 1858, but a compiled map of northern California, incorporating Beechey's San Francisco survey, was issued under Wilkes' name in 1849. (Maps Nos. 24, 25.)

The Beechey charts appeared with Russian titles and text (they were actually copied from the Duflot de Mofras version of the Beechey charts) in at least two instances: (1) the *Map of the bays of Bodega, S. Francisco and Monterey, redrawn by colonial maritime explorers,* and *Entrance into the Bay of San Francisco,* in the M. D. Tebien'kov *Atlas of the northwestern coast of America from Behrings Straits to Cape Corrientes and the Aleutian Islands,* chart 14, 1852 (translated from a copy of the Russian atlas in the Bancroft Library); and (2) the *Harbor of San Francisco in New California, from the English Captain F. W. Beechey, drawn up in the years 1827 and 1828,* and the *Entrance to the Harbor of San Francisco,* in an unidentified Russian atlas probably issued before 1850 (in the Bancroft Library).

Cadwalader Ringgold, a member of the Wilkes expedition of 1841, charted San Francisco Bay and its tributaries in 1849, and copied a large part of his data pertaining to San Francisco Bay from Beechey's well executed survey. The general chart and sheets Nos. 1 and 2 in his *A series of*

1827-1828
Frederick William Beechey

1827/1828 Frederick William Beechey

charts and sailing directions, 1851 (charts dated 1850) show his considerable debt to Beechey. In return, the 1851 edition of Beechey's chart, issued by the English Hydrographical Office, apparently borrowed "The Sacramento from an American map" from sheet No. 3 of the Ringgold series. Ringgold's chart, and through it Beechey's, was also appropriated and published, much reduced, in Henry Lange's *Atlas von Nord-America,* 1854 (plate 18).

The English publisher James Imray used Beechey's two bay charts as insets in his *Chart of the coast of California from San Blas to San Francisco,* 1851. They were probably taken from the printed Hydrographical Office edition of 1833, for the three rivers beyond Carquinez Strait appear.

The British Hydrographical Office published a revised edition of the two charts of the bay in 1851 as Admiralty chart, *America, West Coast,* No. 591, with the note, "Published . . . March 20th 1833. Additions to 1851." The addition was chiefly the Sacramento River, which replaced the reputed river system previously shown. This revision seems to have been taken over from Ringgold's 1849 survey as presented in his *Chart of Suisun & Vallejo bays with the confluence of the rivers Sacramento and San Joaquin,* dated 1850. (In Ringgold, *A series of charts and sailing directions,* 1851, sheet 3. The Suisun chart was also issued separately as early as March 1850; see the San Francisco *Alta California,* March 26, 1850, p. 2, col. 4.)

The Beechey influence upon San Francisco Bay charts persisted for many years, but we need not pursue it further. The best early maps of the California gold region reflected it (directly or through Duflot de Mofras or American copies), for many of them included the bay, gateway to the mines. Beechey's work, as amended by Wilkes and Ringgold, was but gradually outmoded by the cumulative investigations of the U. S. Coast and Geodetic Survey.

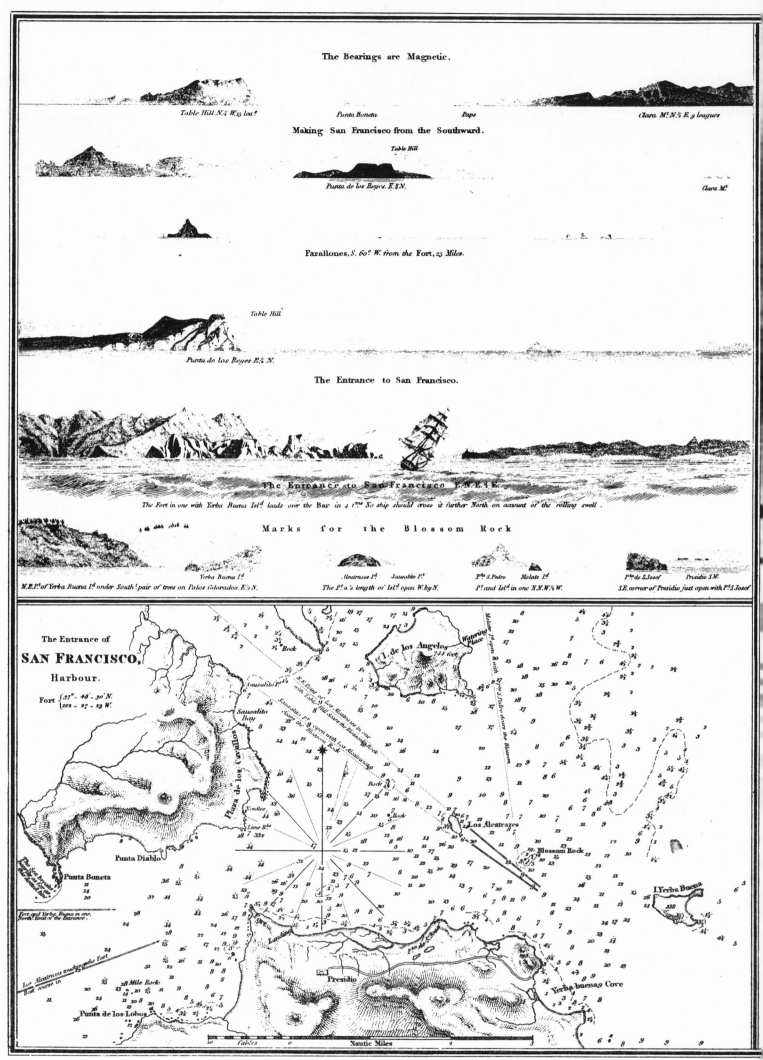

The Bearings are Magnetic.

Table Hill N.¾ W.15 lea.ᵗ

Punta Boneta   Raps

Clara M.ᵗ N.½ E. 9 leagues

Making San Francisco from the Southward.

Table Hill

Punta de los Reyes. E.¾ N.

Clara M.ᵗ

Farallones, S. 60° W. from the Fort, 25 Miles.

Table Hill

Punta de los Reyes E.¾ N.

The Entrance to San Francisco.

The Entrance to San Francisco E.N.E.¼ E.

The Fort in one with Yerba Buena Isl.ᵈ leads over the Bar in 4 f.ᵐˢ No ship should cross it further North on account of the rolling swell.

Marks for the Blossom Rock

N.E.P.ᵗ of Yerba Buena Isl.ᵈ under South ᵗ pair of trees on Palos Colorados. E.¾ N.

Yerba Buena Iˢˡ.ᵈ

Alcatrazes Iˢˡ.ᵈ   Sausalito P.ᵗ
The P.ᵗ a's length of Iˢˡ.ᵈ open W. by N.

P.ᵗᵃ S. Pedro   Molate Iˢˡ.ᵈ
P.ᵗ and Iˢˡ.ᵈ in one N.N.W.½ W.

P.ᵗᵃ de S. Josef   Presidio S.W.
S.E. corner of Presidio just open with P.ᵗ S. Josef

The Entrance of
SAN FRANCISCO,
Harbour.

Fort { 37° . 48´ . 30´´ N.
       122 .. 27 .. 23 W.

Sausalito P.ᵗ

Sausalito Bay

Plaza de los Cavallos

Punta Diablo

Punta Boneta

Fort and Yerba Buena in one,
North limit of the Entrance.

Los Alcatrazes touching the Fort
Best course in

Punta de los Lobos

Rock

I.ᵈ de los Angeles

Watering Place

Molate I.ᵈ open with
N.ᵗᵉ S. Pedro clear the Blossom

N.E. Point of Los Alcatrazes in one
with Table Hill clears the Blossom Rock

Sausalito P.ᵗ open with Los Alcatrazes
clears the Blossom Rock

Rock

Rock

Lime Rk.ᵃ

Los Alcatrazes

Blossom Rock

I. Yerba Buena

Landing

P.ᵗᵃ de los

Presidio

Yerba buena Cove

Cables   Nautic Miles

London Published according

Maps No. 20 & 21

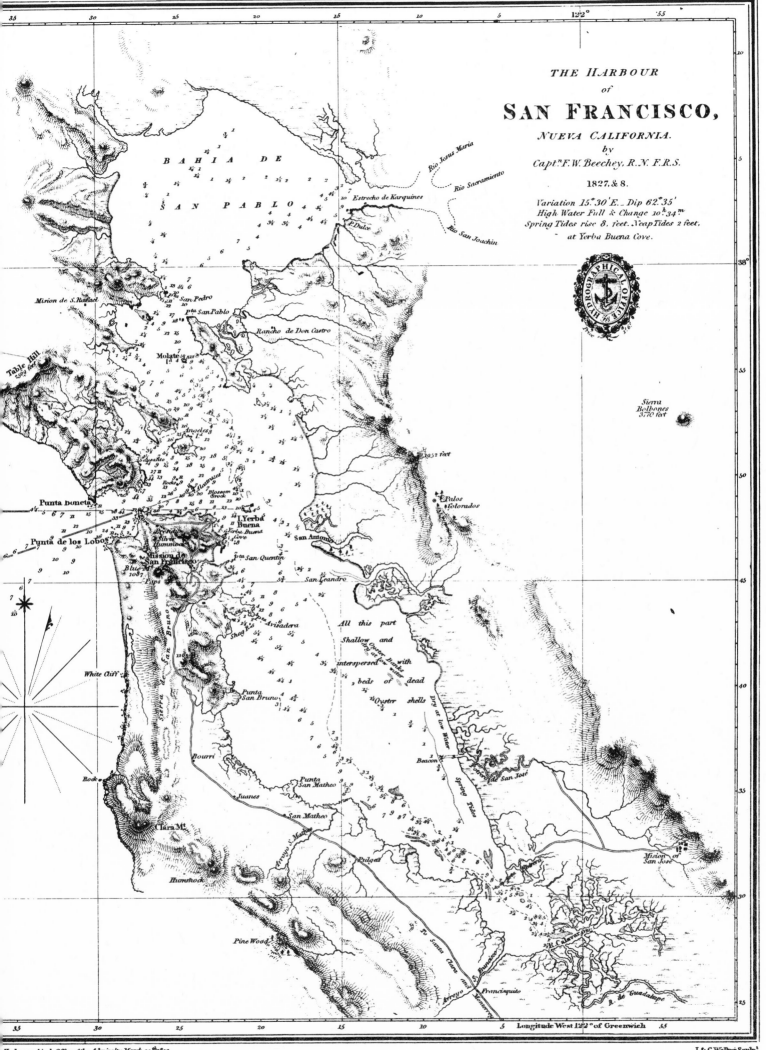

THE HARBOUR
of
SAN FRANCISCO,
NUEVA CALIFORNIA.
by
Capt.ⁿ F. W. Beechey, R. N. F.R.S.
1827, & 8.

Variation 15.°30'E. Dip 62.°35'
High Water Full & Change 10ʰ.34ᵐ
Spring Tides rise 8. feet. Neap Tides 2 feet,
at Yerba Buena Cove.

BAHIA DE
SAN PABLO

Rio Jesus Maria
Rio Sacramiento
Estrecho de Karquines
Rio San Joachin
P. Dulce

Mision de S. Rafael
Pta San Pedro
Pta San Pablo
Rancho de Don Castro
Molate I.ᵈ

Table Hill
580 feet

Sierra
Bolbones
3770 feet

Angel I.ᵈ

1952 feet

Sapanto
Rocks
Alcatrazes
Blossom Rock

Palos
Colorados

Punta Boneta
I. Yerba
Buena
Yerba Buena Cove

Presidio
Silver
Humrock
Mision de
San Francisco
Blue
1007
Paps

San Antonio

Punta de los Lobos

Pta San Quentin

San Leandro

Avisadera
Shag

All this part
Shallow and
interspersed
, beds of dead
Oyster shells

White Cliff

Punta
San Bruno

Beacon

San José

Bourri

Rocks

Punta
San Matheo
Juanes

Clara M.ᵗ

San Matheo

Arroyo S. Matheo

Pulgas

Mision of
San José

Hornhock

Pine Wood

R. Calaveras

R. de Guadalupe
Franciscquito

Hydrographical Office of the Admiralty March 20.ᵗʰ 1833.

J. & C. Walker Sculp.ᵗ

The Harbour of San Francisco, Nueva Califor- 1827-1828
nia, by Captn. F. W. Beechey, R. N. F. R. S. Frederick William
1827, & 8. Beechey

;0 x 25 cm.

"London, Published according to act of Parliament at the Hydro-
graphical office of the Admiralty, March 20th. 1833."
Hydrographical office, chart No. 591.
"Variation 15°. 30′ E. Dip 62°. 35′ High water full & change 10 h.
34 m. Spring tides rise 8, feet. Neap tides 2 feet, at Yerba Buena
Cove."
'J. & C. Walker, Sculpt."
On same sheet: "The entrance of San Francisco Harbour."

>>><<<

THE FIRST printed edition of Beechey's chart of San Francisco Bay, reduced and revised from the original manuscript of 1827–1828. As one of
the series of sailing charts published by the English Hydrographical Office,
it was in general circulation and had a wide influence upon later maps of
the area. The chart, with copies and adaptations of it, served to the end of
the Mexican period and formed the substantial basis of the earliest ones
produced under the American regime. It was deficient only in the region
beyond Carquinez Strait, where the three rivers appended to Beechey's
original survey appeared, an error which was rectified in the subsequent
edition of 1851.

Copies: The one reproduced here is from the Hydrographic Department
of the Admiralty, Bath, England.

Reproductions: Not found.

Listed: Not found.

Additional notes: Two manuscript copies of the 1833 printed edition of
the Beechey chart of San Francisco Bay are preserved among public archives of Contra Costa County at Martinez, California (*Deeds*, v. 10, p.

1827-1828 Frederick William Beechey

161, 175, accompanying a deed from Joaquín G. Castro, *et al*, to George Holmes). It has been supposed that they may have been copies of the manuscript chart left by Beechey with Ignacio Martínez, commandante at San Francisco at the time of Beechey's visit in 1827–1828, but a comparison of the copies with the printed edition of 1833 shows them to have been taken from that source. (A reproduction of the chart appearing at p. 161 of the book of deeds cited above was published in Beechey, *An account of a visit to California*, 1941, p. 50.) The two charts are not complete copies of the printed edition.

The second printed edition of Beechey's chart of the bay was published in 1851. Though amended to include the mouths of the Sacramento and San Joaquin rivers, the new edition was apparently taken from the same, though altered, plate as the 1833 chart. In making the new edition, the original title was removed to provide space for the insertion of Suisun Bay and the river mouths, and a new title was added: *San Francisco Harbour, surveyed by Captn. F. W. Beechey, R. N., F. R. S. 1827–8 . . . The Sacramento from an American map.* (London, Published . . . at the Hydrographical Office of the Admiralty, March 20th. 1833. Additions to 1851.) The 1851 chart bears the Admiralty series note, *America. West coast,* and retains its original number, 591. The "American map" seems to have been sheet number 3 in *A series of charts with sailing directions*, by Cadwalader Ringgold (1851), having the title, *Chart of Suisun & Vallejo bays with the confluence of the rivers Sacramento and San Joaquin*, 1850. The inset chart showing the entrance to San Francisco Bay was reprinted without change.

The entrance of San Francisco Harbour.

13½ x 26 cm.

"London, Published . . . at the Hydrographical office of the Admiralty, March 20th. 1833."
"Fort: 37°. 48'. 30". N. 122°. 27'. 23" W."
On same sheet with: *The Harbour of San Francisco . . . 1827, & 8.*
Hydrographical office chart No. 591.

≫≫⟨≪≪

A CHART of the entrance of the bay, a detail of Beechey's general chart containing additional hydrographic data pertinent to entering the port and reaching the chief places of anchorage. Accompanying the chart are elevation views depicting the approaches to the bay and the hazards to navigation.

Copies: The 1833 edition of chart No. 591 is found in the Hydrographic Department, Admiralty, London. In the revised edition issued in 1851 no change was made in the chart of the entrance.

Reproductions: Not found.

Listed: Not found.

1833
Frederick William
Beechey

1839
Frederick William Beechey

Geological plan of the Port of San Francisco California. [London, 1839.]

23 x 18½ cm.

"Coloured by Lieut. E. Belcher, R.N., F. G. S."
Inset: view of Needle Rock.

A COLORED geological map based upon Beechey's chart of 1827–1828. It accompanied an article on the geology of San Francisco Bay by A. Collie, published in *The geology of Captain Beechey's voyage*, 1839, by J. Richardson. The area of the map is roughly the tips of the San Francisco and Marin peninsulas and the east bay shore from Point Richmond to San Antonio Creek.

Copies: In Richardson, *The geology of Captain Beechey's voyage*, 1839, plate 3.

Reproductions: Bancroft, *California*, 1886–1890, v. 2, p. 589 (incomplete and not a facsimile).

Listed: Phillips, *California*, No. 192.

Harbour of San Francisco. By Captn. Beechey, R. N. [London, 1839.]

1839
Frederick William Beechey

10 x 13 cm.

≫≫≪≪

A DETAIL of the Beechey chart of San Francisco Bay, including the San Francisco peninsula to south of the mission, a large part of Marin peninsula, and the east shore from Point Pinole south to San Antonio Creek. It is a selective copy, showing the approaches to the bay, soundings, and some surface detail but not the amount of relief found in the original. As published it was accompanied by charts of five other California harbors: Bodega, San Diego, Monterey, Santa Barbara, and San Pedro.

Copies: It appears as an inset on the map of *The coasts of Guatemala and Mexico from Panama to Cape Mendocino, with the principal harbours of California,* 1839, a folding map issued with Forbes, *California; a history,* 1839.

Reproductions: Reprinted with the modern editions of Forbes' *California* by T. C. Russell in 1919 and John Henry Nash in 1937.

Listed: Not found.

1841 Map of Sacramento River and Bay of San
U. S. Exploring Pablo with Harbour of San Francisco, by the
Expedition U. S. Ex. Ex. 1841. [Philadelphia, 1858.]

58 x 38½ cm.
Sherman & Smith, printers.
Longitude west of Greenwich.

A CHART produced by the expedition under Charles Wilkes, the first United States exploring expedition in the Pacific.

Charles Wilkes, commander of the U. S. Exploring Expedition, arrived in the Pacific in 1841. In August, at the Columbia River, he dispatched an expedition overland to California and another party by water to San Francisco Bay, arriving there himself in October. A survey of the Sacramento River from its mouth to just beyond the present town of Colusa was carried out, and observations were made in San Pablo and Suisun bays, on the San Joaquin River, and elsewhere about the bay.[1] The chart is dated 1841, the year of the visit to San Francisco, but it was not officially published with the atlas of the expedition until 1858. It included the Sacramento River southward from about the site of Colusa, and the bays of San Pablo and San Francisco down to Hunter's Point. An insert shows the entrance to the harbor.

The charting of the Sacramento was wholly from Wilkes' survey. San Pablo and San Francisco bays and the entrance of the port were modeled upon Beechey's charts, revised to include many new soundings and, particularly in San Pablo Bay, modifications in the shore line.

Copies: Published in U. S. Exploring Expedition. *United States exploring expedition during the years 1838, 1839, 1840, 1841, 1842. Under the command of Charles Wilkes, U. S. N. Atlas of charts*, 1858, v. 2, plate 93. Also issued by the U. S. Coast and geodetic survey as chart No. 161.

Reproductions: Not found.

Listed: Phillips, *Geographical atlases*, No. 3246.

SAN FRANCISCO
BYTHE
U.S. Ex. Ex.
1841.

MAP OF

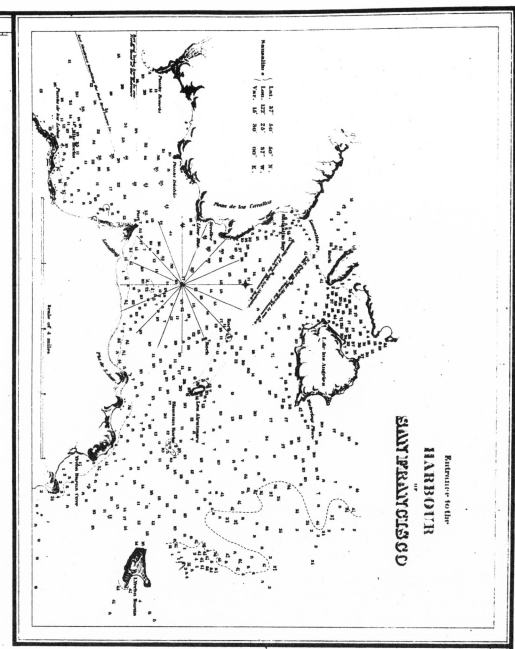

Entrance to the
HARBOUR
OF
SAN FRANCISCO

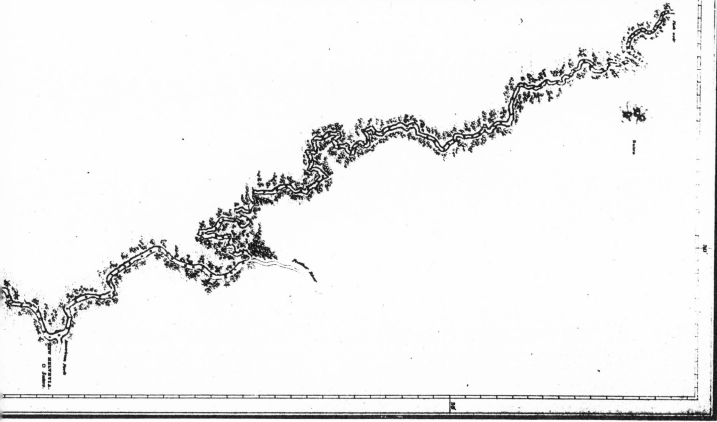

Additional notes: Although the official chart of the Wilkes survey at San Francisco was not published until 1858, a map of 1849 made the data available to the voracious audience of gold seekers. Drawn by F. D. Stuart, *A correct map from actual surveys and examinations embracing a portion of California between Monterey and the Prairie Butes* [!] *in the valley of the Sacramento, shewing the placers* (59 x 42 cm.) was published as a frontispiece to Wilkes, *Western America, including California and Oregon,* 1849. This map included a much wider area than the chart of 1841 and was on a greatly reduced scale.

Cadwalader Ringgold, a member of the Wilkes expedition of 1841, resurveyed the Sacramento River (to the city of Sacramento) and San Francisco Bay in 1849 at the request of San Francisco merchants. His general chart and five detailed sheets were based upon his own work and that of the surveys of Beechey and the U. S. Exploring Expedition. They were drawn by Fred D. Stuart, who executed the map which appeared in Wilkes' *Western America.* The group of charts, dated 1850, with accompanying sailing directions, was published in 1851 as *A series of charts and sailing directions.* Sheet 3, of Suisun Bay, seems to have been sold separately as early as March 1850 (San Francisco *Alta California*, March 26, 1850, p. 2, col. 4), and sheets 1, 2, and 3 were also published by the U. S. Hydrographic Office.

1841
U. S. Exploring Expedition

**1841
U.S. Exploring
Expedition**

Entrance to the Harbour of San Francisco. [Philadelphia, 1858.]

18 x 22 ½ cm.

Scale in miles.

Inset on the expedition's *Map of Sacramento River and Bay of San Pablo.*

→→→←←←

THE CHART is a revision of the *Entrance of San Francisco Harbour*, produced by the Beechey expedition of 1827–1828. Additional soundings were supplied, and some which Beechey had recorded were eliminated. The presidio and the road to Yerba Buena Cove do not appear, and the latitude and longitude of Sausalito, where Wilkes' ship lay, was substituted for Beechey's calibrations for Fort Point.

Copies: In U. S. Exploring expedition. *United States Exploring expedition during the years 1838, 1839, 1840, 1841, 1842. . . . Atlas of charts,* 1858, v. 2, inset on plate 93.

Reproductions: Not found.

Listed: As U. S. Exploring expedition chart 93, listed in Phillips, *Geographical atlases,* No. 3246.

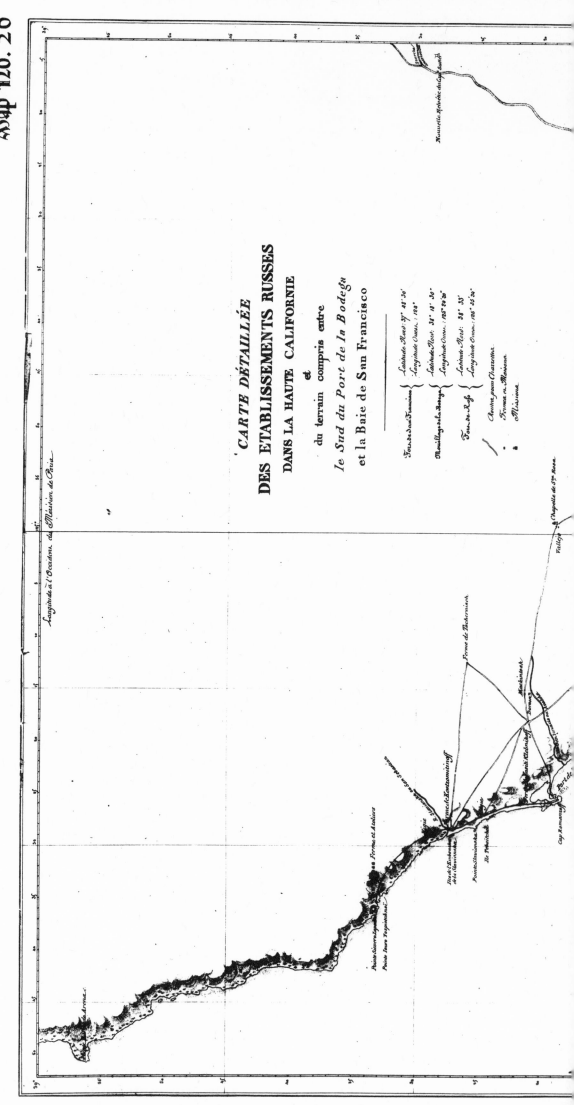

CARTE DÉTAILLÉE
DES ETABLISSEMENTS RUSSES
DANS LA HAUTE CALIFORNIE
et
du terrain compris entre
le Sud du Port de la Bodega
et la Baie de San Francisco

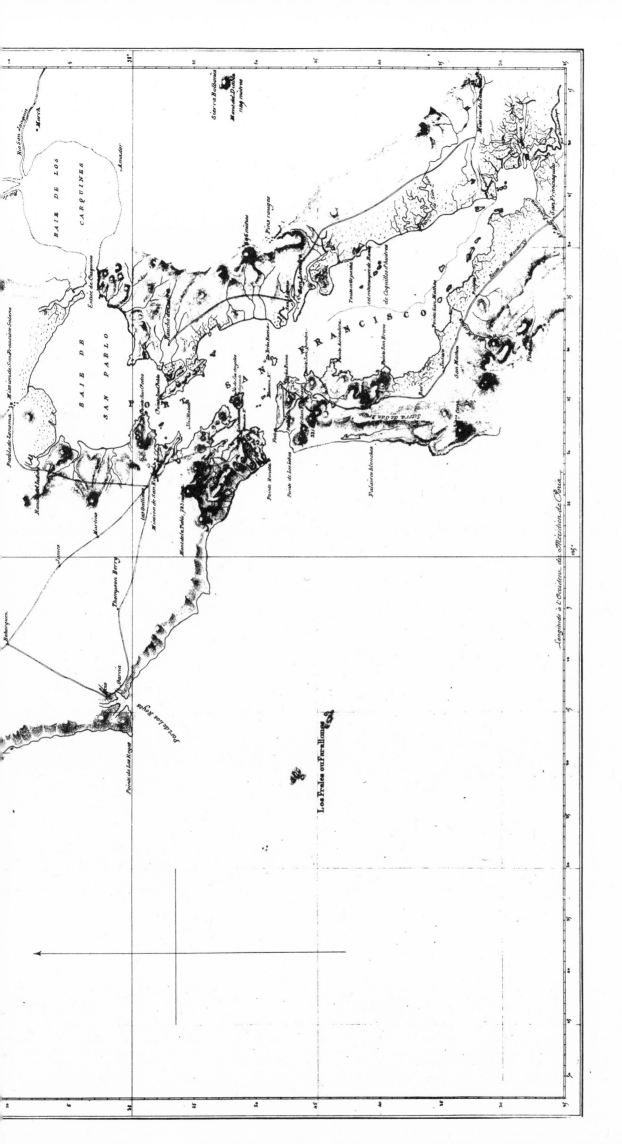

Carte détaillée des établissements russes dans la Haute Californie et du terrain compris entre le sud du Port de la Bodega et la Baie de San Francisco.

1841

Eugène Duflot de Mofras

60 x 49 ½ cm. Manuscript.

The latitude and longitude of the fort at San Francisco, the anchorage at Bodega, and of Fort Ross are given. "Longitude à l'occident du méridien de Paria [!]."

➤➤►◄◄◄

A MAP of the vicinity of San Francisco Bay from Point Arena south to San Francisquito Creek, including a sketch of the Sacramento River northward to Sutter's Fort and the American River. It was made by Duflot de Mofras, who expanded the San Francisco chart of the Beechey survey by incorporating data which he obtained during his visit in 1841.

Eugène Duflot de Mofras, making a semi-official tour of observation on the northwest coast in the French interest, was several times at San Francisco between May and October 1841 and traveled to many points about the bay and into the interior. His published account, including the atlas, comprised his own observations and a vast amount of data obtained from other sources. In his text he fully acknowledged his debt to Beechey for the plan of San Francisco Bay, presumably the Hydrographical Office edition of 1833, and Beechey's work is probably as well known in this modified French edition as in the original English. Like Beechey's charts, the 1844 published map of Duflot de Mofras was a favorite source among later mapmakers.[1]

In adapting the Beechey chart to his use, Duflot de Mofras had the original redrawn, the text translated into French, and the soundings and elevations changed into meters. For Beechey's three rivers he substituted an oval Baie de los Carquines of indeterminate size, at the eastern end of which he drew the San Joaquin and Sacramento rivers and an alternate

1841
Eugène Duflot de Mofras

mouth of the latter named the Jesus María. The latter feature was a skillful solution by an eye witness of the old riddle of the Jesus María. Among other additions to the map were the Mission de San Francisco Solano, the "Pueblo de Zonoma," the name of Monte de Diablo, the settlements of Marsh, Murphy, and other foreigners, routes of travel north of the bay, and, of course, the whole section between Point Reyes and Point Arena, including the Russian establishments. The map was neatly and handsomely executed with pen and ink.

Copies: Included in Duflot de Mofras, *Mélanges*, v. 2.

Reproductions: Not found.

Listed: Not found.

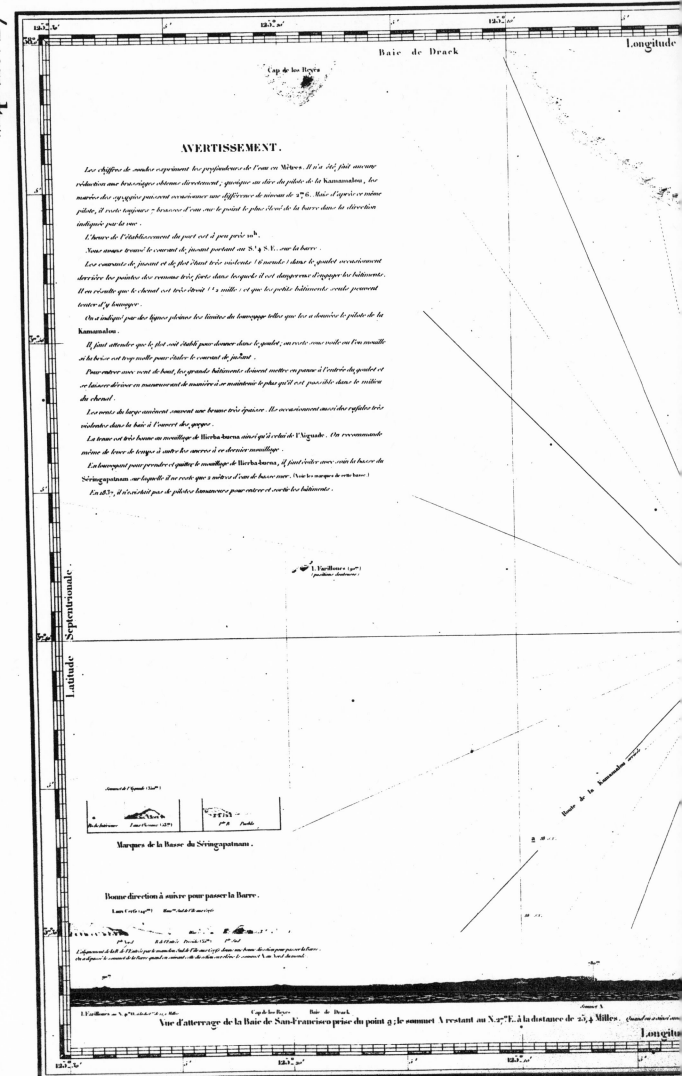

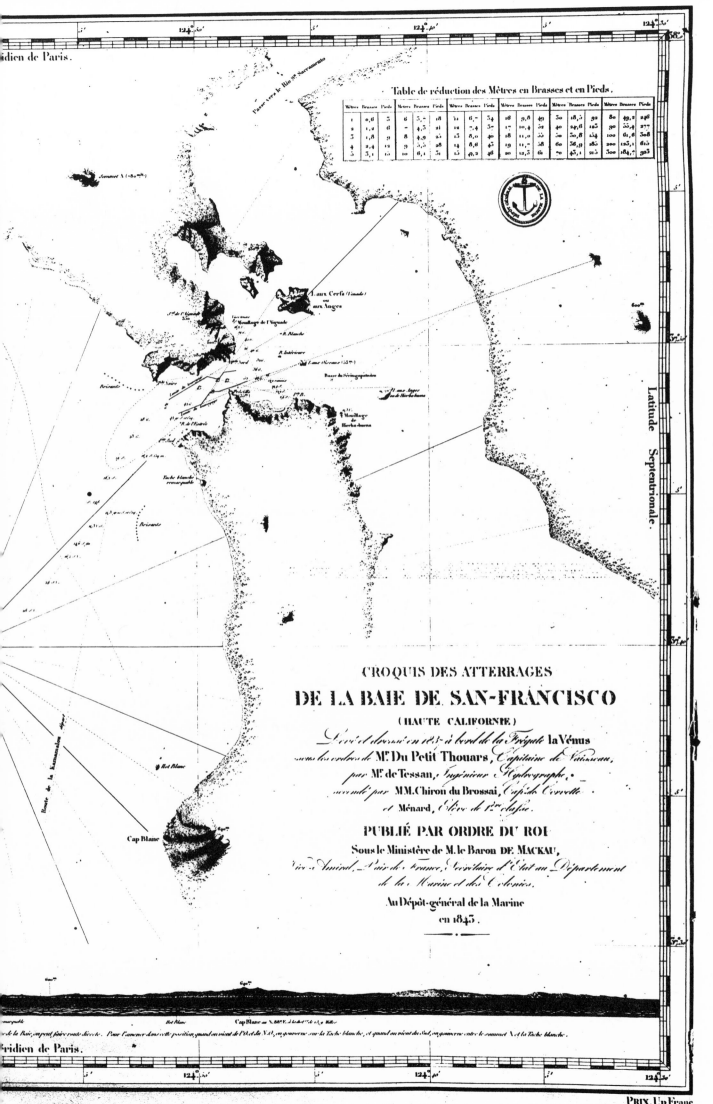

Croquis des atterrages de la Baie de San-Fran- 1843
cisco (Haute Californie). Levé et dressé en 1837 Abel Aubert
à bord de la frégate la Vénus sous les ordres de Dupetit-Thouars
Mr. Du Petit Thouars, capitaine de vaisseau,
par Mr. de Tessan, ingénieur hydrographe, se-
condé par MM. Chiron du Brossai, cap. de cor-
vette et Ménard, elève de 1ère classe. Publié par
ordre du roi sous le ministère de M. le Baron de
Mackau . . . [Paris] Au dépot-général de la
marine en 1843.

39½ x 56½ cm.
"Gravé par Jacobs." "Ecrit par J. M. Hacq."
"Longitude occidentale du méridien de Paris."
Below: elevation view of approaches to San Francisco.
At left: textual explanation and sailing directions.

>>><<<

A CHART of the entrance to San Francisco Bay made by members of the
French expedition under Dupetit-Thouars in October 1837.

  Abel Aubert Dupetit-Thouars, while making investigations in the
Pacific in behalf of French trading interests, dropped anchor in Monterey
harbor on October 18, 1837, and remained there with the frigate *Vénus*
until November 14th. Taking advantage of the presence of the Hawaiian
vessel, the *Kamamalu*, in port, he chartered it to send a party to San Francisco Bay to obtain water and make observations. They remained there
from October 26 to November 1, preparing a chart of the approaches to
the bay (including the Farallones and Point Reyes) and the islands and

1843
Abel Aubert
Dupetit-Thouars

shore line in the vicinity of the entrance. On the chart Yerba Buena Cove is shown as the place of anchorage, modern Yerba Buena or Goat Island being named "I. aux Anges ou de Hierba Buena." Angel Island was called "I. aux Cerfs (Venado) ou Anges" (Deer or Angel Island), while Alcatraz became "I. aux Oiseaux," and Blossom Rock, discovered by Beechey in 1827, was labeled "Basse du Séringapatnam," a name presumably borrowed for the occasion from the island-town in India. Richardson's Bay is appropriately called "Mouillage de l'Aiguade" (Anchorage at the Watering Place), and the height above Sausalito is the "S[omm]et de l'Aiguade." The chart, in keeping with the purposes of the voyage, was intended to serve the cause of commerce, and it included only features which would be useful to navigation.[1] It was published by the French government in the official atlas of the voyage.

Copies: In the *Atlas hydrographique, rédigé par U. de Tessan,* 1845, plate 6 (1002), accompanying Dupetit-Thouars, *Voyage autour du monde sur la frégate la Vénus,* 1840–1844.

Reproductions: Not found.

Listed: Phillips, *Geographical atlases,* No. 205.

[28]

Port de San Francisco dans la Haute Californie. [Paris, 1844.]

1844
Eugène Duflot
de Mofras

29½ x 24½ cm.

"Fort. Latitude nord 37° 48′ 30″. Longitude ouest 124° 48′ 26‴"
"Longitude a l'ouest du méridien de Paris."
"Gravé par S. Jacobs." "Publié par Arthus Bertrand."

A PRINTED chart of San Francisco Bay accompanying the *Exploration du territoire de l'Orégon*, by Eugène Duflot de Mofras, published in 1844.

The chart is a transcription into French of the 1833 edition of Beechey's *San Francisco Harbour, 1827–1828*, revised to include information obtained by Duflot de Mofras during his visit in 1841. Beechey's conjectured three rivers were replaced by an oval Baie de los Carquines, into which were shown to flow only the rivers Sacramento and San Joaquin, the short Rio Jesus María which appeared in the Duflot de Mofras manuscript map of 1841 having been now eliminated. The northward extension of the map of 1841 beyond Beechey's survey was likewise excised from the chart of 1844, most of this region having been incorporated by Duflot de Mofras into a separate chart.[1] At the time of the California gold rush the Duflot de Mofras and Beechey charts of the bay were eagerly seized by publishers ready to pirate any material pertaining to this popular area.

Copies: Duflot de Mofras, *Exploration du territoire de l'Orégon, des Californies et de la Mer Vermeille. Atlas*, 1844, plate 16.

Reproductions: Not found.

Listed: Phillips, *California*, No. 197.

29

1844
Eugène Duflot
de Mofras

Entrée du Port de San Francisco et des mouil-
lages del Sausalito et de la Yerba Buena. [Paris,
1844.]

13 x 24½ cm.

"Gravé par S. Jacobs."

Printed on the same sheet with Duflot de Mofras' chart of the *Port de San Francisco*.

THE CHART is a revision, in French, of Beechey's *Entrance of San Francisco Harbour* of 1827–1828, taken from the printed edition of 1833. Duflot de Mofras' additions to Beechey's survey were the location of William A. Richardson's house at Sausalito, the extension of the road from the San Francisco presidio to Fort Point, and a representation of the settlement of Yerba Buena, showing the location of buildings.

Copies: In Duflot de Mofras, *Exploration du territoire de l'Orégon, des Californies et de la Mer Vermeille. Atlas*, 1844, bottom of plate 16.

Reproductions: Not found.

Listed: Phillips, *California*, No. 197.

THE MAPS OF THE
TOWN OF
SAN FRANCISCO

1835-1847

30

[Preliminary sketch of a plan of the town of Yerba Buena. May, 1835.]

1835

William Antonio Richardson

Manuscript.

THE FIRST plan of the town of Yerba Buena, later the city of San Francisco, drawn by Richardson at the request of Governor José Figueroa in May 1835.

Yerba Buena Cove, the "most excellent small bay" mentioned by Vancouver, had been a place of anchorage at least since Vancouver's visit in 1792.[1] It later became more popular with merchantmen than the official anchorage below the presidio, for it offered a better holding ground and afforded greater protection from wind and wave. Probably its very distance from the presidio added to its attractiveness. The beach was not a good landing place but was shallow and could only be approached by ships' boats at high tide, usually at the north end. Its general use dated from December 1824 when strong ebb tides, resulting from unusually heavy freshets from the rivers, made the old exposed anchorage dangerous. Not until 1828, however, did the governor officially countenance the anchorage of vessels in the cove, but Roquefeuil probably stopped there in 1817, Kotzebue in 1824, Morrell the next year, Beechey in 1826, Duhaut-Cilly in 1827, and many another vessel until trespassing wharves and dirt fills brought about its complete obliteration.[2]

William Antonio Richardson, an English sailor, left the whaler *Orion* at San Francisco on August 2, 1822, and, though a foreigner, was permitted to remain in the country because of his competency as navigator and builder. He was baptized the next year, and in 1825 married a daughter of Ignacio Martínez, commandante of the presidio, and requested land at Yerba Buena. He became a Mexican citizen in 1830, served as Captain of the Port from 1835 to 1844, was bricklayer, surgeon, and carpenter, mended boats, was pilot and interpreter, and for several years carried on a freight and lighterage business in the bay. He resided at the San Francisco

1835
William Antonio Richardson

presidio from 1822 to 1829, at San Gabriel until 1835, from July 1835 to June 1841 at Yerba Buena, and from that time until his death in 1856 at Sausalito.[3]

In November 1834, prior to Richardson's appointment as Captain of the Port, Governor Figueroa ordered the establishment of civil government for the jurisdiction of San Francisco to supplant the existing military administration of political affairs. The *ayuntamiento*, elected on December 7, 1834, and installed the following month, was to govern the peninsula and the east bay ranchos.[4] For some time there had been agitation by Richardson and others to set up a pueblo in the vicinity of the Yerba Buena anchorage, and Governor Figueroa had determined to lay out a town for the convenience of public offices and shipping. In May 1835, while Richardson was at San Gabriel, he was questioned by the governor concerning the place, and he made a sketch map of it for the use of Figueroa and the Territorial Assembly. This map showed the cleared space abreast of Yerba Buena Cove and indicated the lay of the land. It depicted the valley running some 1200 yards in a northwest to southeast direction between the Loma Alta (Telegraph Hill) and the Rincon, and extending from the beach into the sand hills a distance of 400 varas. From Richardson's description of the plan, it would seem to have included no streets or boundary lines.[5]

Copies: Unknown; what purports to be a tracing of a map dated May 1835 appears in Burns, *Centennial of the city of San Francisco*, 1935, p. 6. As this, however, shows the limits of the government reserve, the Calle de la Fundación, and the site of Richardson's lot, all of which were presumably established the following October, it seems likely that it was of a later date.

Reproductions: None found.

Listed: Not found.

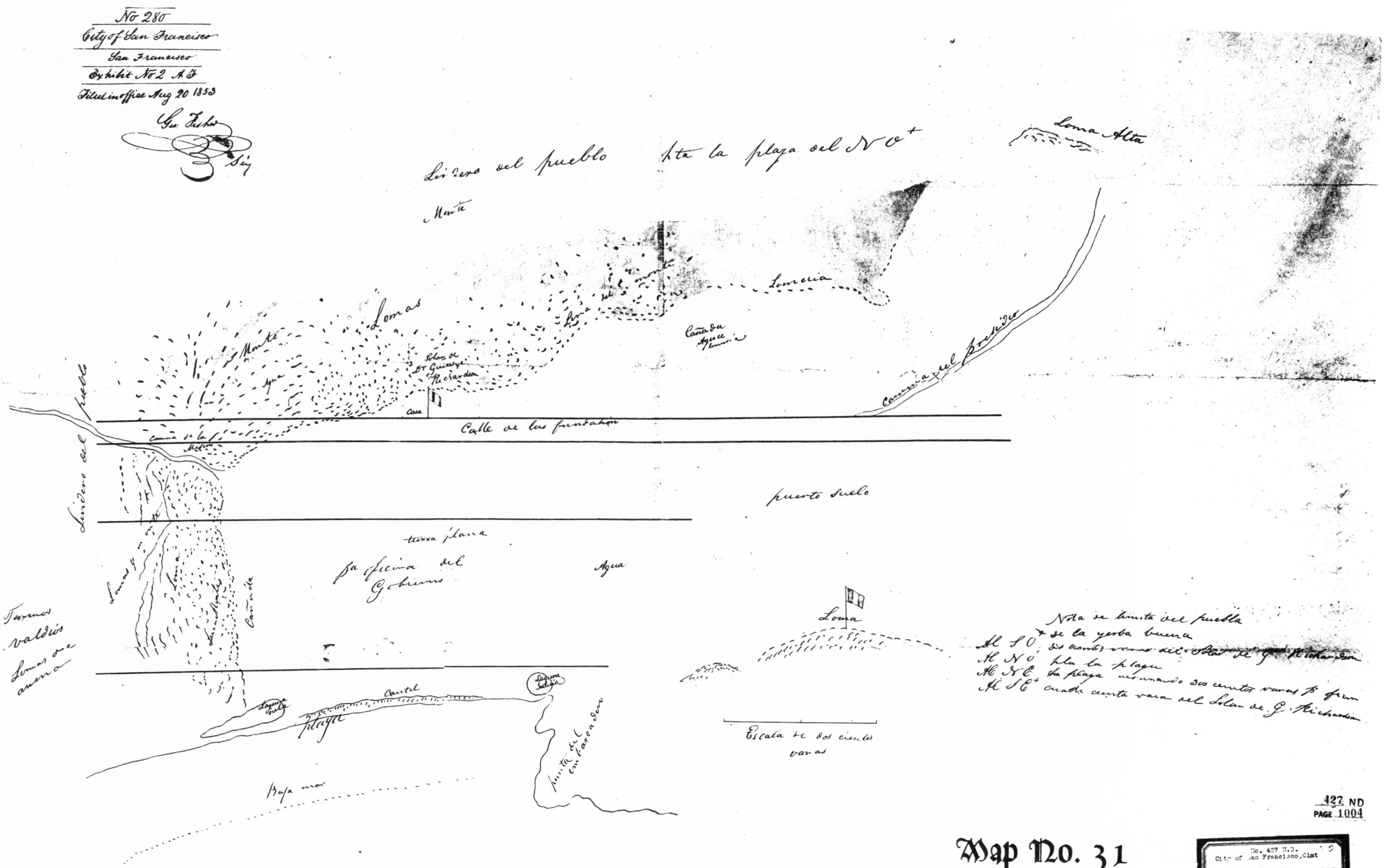
No 280
City of San Francisco
San Francisco
Exhibit No 2 A F
Filed in office Aug 20 1853
Geo. Fisher
Sey
Lindero del pueblo
hta la playa del NO
Loma Alta
Monte
Lomas
Lomeria
Cañada
Solar de Dr Guillermo Richardson
Casa
Camino del Presidio
Calle de las fundacion
puerto suelo
tierra plana
La oficina del Gobierno
Agua
Lindero del pueblo
Terrenos valdios
Lomas de arena
Cañada
Loma
Cantil
Playa
Punta del embarcadero
Baja mar
Escala de dos cientos varas
Nota de limite del pueblo de la yerba buena

Map No. 31

⟫⟫⟫⟫⟫[31]⟪⟪⟪⟪⟪⟪

[Plan of Yerba Buena. October, 1835.]

Manuscript.

⟫⟫⟩⟨⟨⟨

1835
William Antonio
Richardson

THE FIRST official plan of the town of Yerba Buena, drawn by the town's first resident. It was made early in October 1835 and was approved by the governor on October 20.

In June 1835, after Richardson had submitted his sketch map of the proposed town to Governor Figueroa, he set out with his family for Yerba Buena to become Captain of the Port of San Francisco. In October, at the behest of José Castro, the succeeding governor, he assisted Alcalde Francisco de Haro and the *ayuntamiento* to lay out the boundaries of the new town and made a new map of the place. This plan depicted the shore of the cove, the general shape of the terrain, and the approaches to the mission and presidio. An area two hundred varas deep fronting on the beach was set aside as government land, and a hundred varas beyond this appeared a single street, the Calle de la Fundación, along the far side of which was shown the site of Richardson's own lot. The map resembled the typical *diseño* which, according to contemporary Mexican law, must accompany a petition to the government for a private grant of land; and the town was laid out upon the ground in the informal manner characteristic of the time. No compass was used, and the angular direction of the Calle de la Fundación in relation to the streets which were afterwards surveyed parallel to the waterfront (see the Vioget map of 1839) probably was a result of this lack of instruments. Richardson kept the original plan and made another for the governor, which was certified on October 20, 1835, as the official map of Yerba Buena.[1]

Copies: The original map made by Richardson in October 1835 was still in his possession in 1854 and appeared as Exhibit No. 2, A. F. in U. S. District Court case, *U. S.* vs. *Limantour,* and as Exhibit No. 1, A. F. in *The city of San Francisco* vs. *the United States* before the U. S. Land Commis-

1835
William Antonio Richardson

sion. Richardson testified that he made a copy for the governor immediately after drawing the original and that he made several others for the governor at various times, one having been sent to him in 1843.[2] The original is said to have been in recent years in the possession of the late Tom P. Burns of San Francisco.[3] Copies are in the archives of the U. S. District Court for the northern district of California, San Francisco, being maps 919 and 920, accompanying District Court case 427 ND.

Reproductions: In Eldredge, *The beginnings of San Francisco,* 1915, v. 2, p. 504 (not a facsimile).

Listed: Not found.

32

[Plan of Yerba Buena, 1839?]

8½ x 13 cm. Manuscript.

⇶⇶⇷⇷⇷

A PLAN showing the location of the town lots (*solares*) granted by Governor Alvarado to Jacob P. Leese and Salvador Vallejo on May 21, 1839.

During the Mexican regime in California the law providing for the distribution of public land to citizens of the country prescribed that the applicant address a petition to the governor, accompanied by a map, or *diseño*, showing the location of the desired tract and its relation to landmarks in the vicinity. If the specified land proved to be available, and no legal objections were found by the governor to making the grant, a title was issued over the governor's signature, recorded in the official *toma de razón*, and delivered to the grantee, who—awaiting the approval of the territorial *diputación*—was expected to occupy and improve the land within twelve months. A copy of the *diseño*, with other official papers relating to the grant, was deposited in the government archives, while the grantee's title and another copy of the plan remained in his possession as evidence of ownership. Governor Alvarado, in reply to a request from Leese and Vallejo for land upon which to erect buildings and a wharf to accommodate trade with the Russians, issued to the petitioners two one-hundred-vara lots "on the point by the embarcadero of Yerba Buena," at what was later to be known as Clark's Point. A map showing the location of the lots within the town is still preserved in a collection of Leese papers.

Jacob P. Leese, an Ohioan who had engaged in the Santa Fe trade, first came to California in December 1833, stopping at Los Angeles. For a time thereafter he was occupied in driving mules from California to New Mexico, then in 1836 he formed a partnership with Nathan Spear and William S. Hinckley to set up a commercial house in the vicinity of San Francisco Bay. From Governor Chico he secured title to a lot in Yerba Buena adjoining William A. Richardson's on the south—the second grant in the town—

1839
Jacob Primer Leese

and began in July 1836 to erect the first permanent building in the place. Other lots were issued to him, including a store site near the beach on present-day Montgomery Street, and the tract which he owned jointly with Vallejo; and he became the claimant for several Mexican-California ranchos. He was naturalized under Mexican law in September 1836, and the next year he married Rosalía Vallejo, sister of Salvador, their daughter being the first white child born in Yerba Buena. A partner of Spear and Hinckley from 1836, he carried on his own business from 1838 to 1841, and then sold to the Hudson's Bay Company. Leese was active both in business and in public life and was for more than twenty years prominent in California affairs. He participated in an unsuccessful land speculation in Lower California in the 1860s and quit California. A quarter of a century later he returned to San Francisco, suffered a severe injury in 1890, and died in that city on February 1, 1892, at the age of 82.[1]

The map here described follows roughly the plan of Yerba Buena outlined by William A. Richardson in 1835.[2] It shows the boundaries of the town, beginning at the cove "south of a small lake which was on the beach," extending southwesterly two hundred varas beyond the street called Calle de la Fundación, and continuing in a northwesterly direction parallel to this street to the future North Beach. The site of Richardson's lot is indicated, as are the Playa de Juana Briones (named after a widely known resident of the vicinity), Telegraph Hill (unnamed), Rincon Point, the mission road, and the plots held by Castañares, Leese, and Vallejo. On the Richardson map of 1835 the district in the vicinity of the Leese-Vallejo *solares* is labeled "Punta del Embarcadero," and this identification was used to locate the lots in the grant. In 1847, under American jurisdiction, the property was reissued by city officials to others, and a prolonged lawsuit ensued, involving Leese and William S. Clark as principals, terminating in 1866 with Leese victorious.

It is not clearly established that the map here discussed was the *diseño* accompanying the Leese-Vallejo petition. No map is mentioned in contemporary documents, and opposing counsel in the lawsuit declared that the grant to Leese and Vallejo comprised nothing but a petition and the preliminary title issued by the governor, there having been no map attached to the documents, and no survey or other evidence that the claimants had been put in legal possession of the property. The boundaries of the grant, which should have been surveyed by Mexican authorities to complete the title, were not established upon the ground until 1857, when the work was done by the U. S. Surveyor General. Whatever the authority of the plan, it is notable as a map of Yerba Buena because it shows the boundaries of the town which were described by Richardson and were implied in his plan of 1835 but were not actually depicted upon copies of it which have survived.[3]

Copies: The plan here reproduced is part of a collection of Leese papers in the possession of Thomas W. Norris, Carmel, California.

Reproductions: As the *Plan of Yerba Buena*, it was issued in facsimile at Christmas 1946 by Thomas W. Norris.

Listed: Not found.

1839
Jacob Primer
Leese

1839
Jean Jacques
Vioget

Plan of Yerba Buena. 1839.

Manuscript.

➤➤❯❮❮❮

THE FIRST map of San Francisco based upon a formal survey.

After the establishment of the town of Yerba Buena in 1835, requests for *solares* (town lots) were made. William A. Richardson received the first grant on June 2, 1836, and Jacob P. Leese secured an adjoining lot on the following July 8th. By mid-1839 eight grants had been issued[1] without regard to any street system, except for the single Calle de la Fundación which had been established but not surveyed in 1835. Governor Alvarado deemed it expedient to have an adequate plan drawn up, and Alcalde Francisco Guerrero employed Vioget to carry out the work.

Jean Jacques Vioget, a Swiss-French engineer, surveyor, and sailor, traded along the California coast from 1837 to 1839 as master of the Ecuadorian brig *Dalmira*. He resided at Yerba Buena from 1839 to 1843, was naturalized and secured lots there in 1840, married a daughter of the country, built a house, engaged in trade, practiced civil engineering, kept a billiard saloon, later a hotel, and from 1843 to 1848, as master of several ships, made voyages to Mexico, South America, and the Sandwich Islands. From 1849 he lived at San Jose and died there in October 1855. He was something of an artist as well as an engineer and had a reputation as a great eater and drinker and a jolly fellow. His survey of Sutter's New Helvetia ranch was in the courts for many years.[2]

Beginning his survey of Yerba Buena with what is now Montgomery Street, then at the waterfront, Vioget laid off about three blocks westward, four from north to south between present day Sacramento and Pacific streets, and one oversize lot at the south end between what are now Sacramento and California. The original Calle de la Fundación was incorporated into the new scheme,[3] although it did not conform to the direction of the other streets. None of the streets was named, and, curiously, the intersections of the cross streets on the plan were made about two and a half

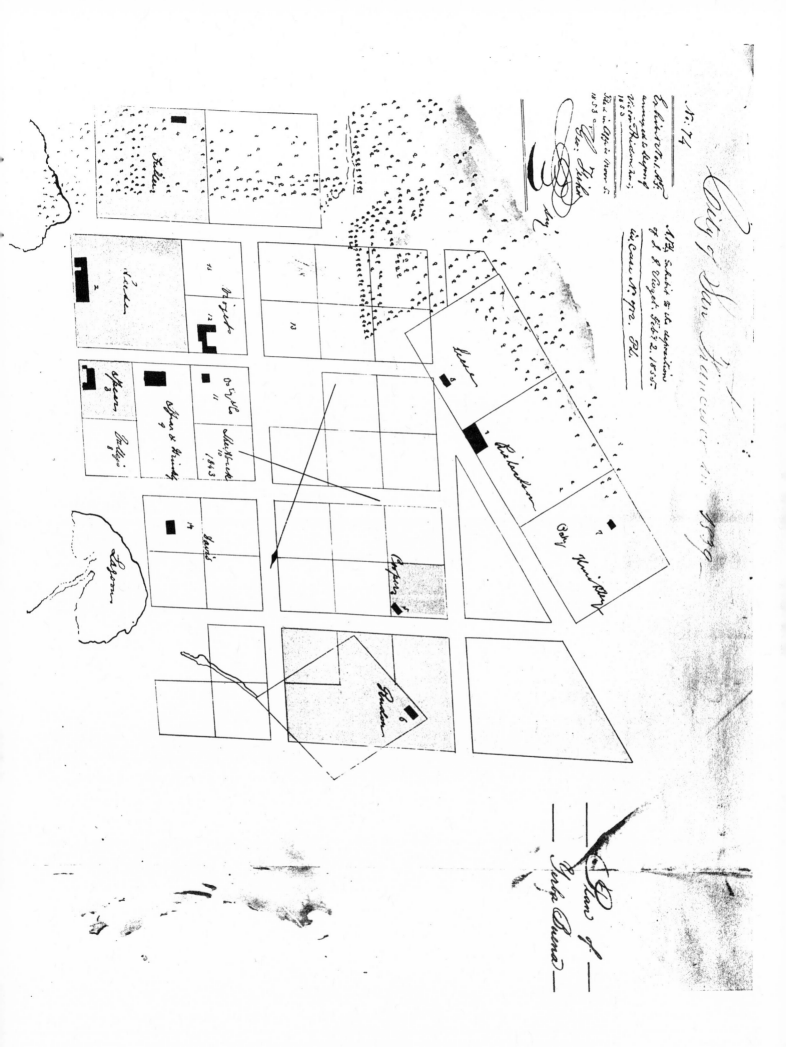

Map No. 33

degrees from a right angle. Vioget's north later proved to be eleven degrees too far east. Vioget stated that he received no instructions regarding the limits of the town but that he drew the map to embrace the houses and fences already erected, making dotted lines to suggest that extensions of the streets might later be made. Ownership of lots was indicated on the map, which was completed in about November 1839.

Copies: The location of the original, which was sent to the governor, is not now known; copies introduced as evidence in several California land cases are found in the U. S. District Court archives, San Francisco (maps 905, 912, 921). A colored facsimile is in the archives of the Secretary of State of California, Sacramento, in *U. S. vs. Limantour. Photographic exhibits,* 1858, part 12. No located copy exhibits the dotted lines showing the extension of the streets, as described in Vioget's testimony, and all show the Plaza to embrace but a single 50-vara lot.[4]

Reproductions: Eldredge, *History of California,* 1915, v. 2, p. 512 (not a facsimile).

Listed: Not found.

Additional notes: Upon the extant copies of Vioget's plan, fourteen grants of lots are shown to have been made, and these indicate that the latest use of the map must have been in 1842. The Sherreback lot, dated 1843 on the copies, was actually issued on May 1, 1842. The dates of the grants, as taken from schedules "A" and "E" of Alfred Wheeler's *Land titles in San Francisco,* 1852, are as follows: 1836—Richardson; Leese. 1837—Paty and Hinckley (granted to Hinckley); Fuller. 1838—Prudon (to Caseres). 1839—Spear and Hinckley (to Hinckley); Davis. 1840—Cooper; Vioget; Leese; J. A. Vallejo; Spear. [1841—none.] 1842—Paty & Co. (to Allen); Sherreback.

1839
Jean Jacques Vioget

[34]

1843
Anonymous

[Map of the town of Yerba Buena. c. 1843.]

Manuscript.

IT IS difficult, and perhaps impossible, at this time to establish with certainty the identity of the maps of Yerba Buena which may have been made between 1839 and 1847 (between the Vioget and "Alcalde" maps). The last town lot granted according to the Vioget plan of 1839, or at least the last noted upon extant copies of it, was issued on May 1, 1842, and it would seem, therefore, that a new map came into use sometime between May 1842 and April 1843, when a new series of grants was made. The first town lot to be taken up outside the limits of the Vioget survey was issued on December 15, 1843, and another lot granted the same day was the first to have a lot number noted in the grant. If a regular scheme of numbering lots was inaugurated at this time, it is possible to ascertain the area of the plan then in use. Observing the order in which the numbers were arranged, it is seen that the first 180 lots comprised an oblong bounded by Montgomery and Vallejo streets and a line two-thirds of a block west of present-day Mason Street and a half block south of California. It was more than a coincidence that no grants were made outside this area until 1846 and that the next enlargement of the plan of the town (an extension to include lots numbered up to 360) comprised the area of the Bartlett map of 1846–1847.[1]

At this time, or perhaps earlier, the streets upon the plan were apparently realigned to intersect at right angles, and the diagonal Calle de la Fundación was eliminated. Washington A. Bartlett testified in 1864 that a realignment of the streets was effected by members of the Wilkes expedition, which, if true, must have occurred during August to October 1841, and suggests that another map may have been in use during 1842 and 1843. There is great confusion in testimony taken in later years regarding the identity and appearance of the "old map" of Yerba Buena, and this is not remarkable, for the appearance of each revised map automatically relegated its predecessor to that category. The map here provisionally dated 1843 was probably the "first map of surveyed land" mentioned by John Henry Brown and said by him to have hung in Robert Ridley's saloon. It may have been the one thought by Eldredge to have been made in 1845 at Captain Hinckley's request upon the authority of the prefect at Monterey. It was probably the map on "coarse brown paper" which Bartlett remembered as having no title and no street names, upon which the lots known or thought to have been granted were numbered and, often, labeled with the names of the grantees. It may even have been the map said by T. M. Leavenwourth, Samuel Short, and others to have been marked "Plan of Yerba Buena, 1846," its title and date having been affixed in 1847, perhaps, to differentiate it from its successor. A "plano de la Yerba Buena reformado" is known to have been in existence in 1845, for it is recorded in an *Inventory of all the archives from the foundation of the Ayuntamiento* [of San Francisco] *in 1835, to the end of the present year* [1845]. It may also be possible that under the entry of 1843 we have not only lumped an earlier map of 1841 or 1842 but in addition one or more later ones of 1844 or 1845; the available evidence is unfortunately insufficient to refute or confirm these suppositions.[2]

Copies: No fully authenticated copy known; Burns had a tracing of a plan which he dated November 1843, but its source is not known (Burns, *Centennial of the city of San Francisco,* 1935, p. 12). The original may have been the old framed map which hung in the Recorder's office in San Francisco and was destroyed in the fire of 1906.

Reproductions: We have only the unauthenticated copy presented by Burns, cited above.

Listed: Not found.

1843
Anonymous

1846
John Henry Brown

[Plan of Yerba Buena. 1846.]

Manuscript.

A COPY of the "first map of surveyed land" which according to John Henry Brown was made by Captain William J. Hinckley and himself sometime prior to July 1846.

Brown, a British sailor, wandered across the continent to California in 1843 and finally settled in Yerba Buena in January 1846. In February he took charge of Robert Ridley's liquor and billiard saloon (later the Portsmouth House, near the corner of Clay and Kearny streets), which had come to be the informal meeting place of the town. Back of the bar, Brown stated, hung the "first map of surveyed land," and upon it were written the numbers of the town lots and, as lots were granted, the names of the owners. By 1846 the map had become much soiled and tattered, and William Hinckley, Captain of the Port, offered to make a copy of it, but, according to Brown, was too nervous to draw the necessary lines. Brown then completed the map under Hinckley's supervision, and it was substituted for the old map, which was put away for safe keeping. The Brown map hung in the bar room until sometime after the raising of the American flag in July 1846 when Washington A. Bartlett secured it for the municipal government.[1]

Except for some doubtful references to this map, the fact of its existence rests largely upon Brown's testimony. Eldredge considered the Brown plan, or its predecessor, and Bartlett's revision of 1847 to have been the same map, and this lead has generally been followed by later writers. Brown stated, however, that his copy was made before the American occupation in July 1846, while George Hyde declared the Bartlett revision to have been finished and brought into his office sometime between December 15, 1846, and January 20, 1847, adding that "We used to call it the Buckalew map, because Buckalew made it." Whether the Brown map was the original from which the Bartlett map was made is also debatable. Brown remembered that the "old map" was put away for safe keeping after his copy was hung in its place back of the bar and that both were surrendered to Bartlett after the raising of the American flag. Bartlett's testimony mentioned only a single plan of the town, "on coarse brown paper," which he received from Alcalde Noé with the town archives. Since T. M. Leavenwourth and Samuel Short described the old map as having the title "Plan of Yerba Buena, 1846," and George Hyde said it had street names, though incorrect (he may have had it confused with the Bartlett copy which had this defect), it is possible that Brown's copy was the particular "old map" remembered by so many men of 1847—for the map of *circa* 1843 in its original state had neither of these distinguishing characteristics. Whether Brown's 1846 copy was hung in the alcalde's office and was generally remembered as the old map, or whether the older map was given a title and dated 1846 seems impossible to ascertain at this time. One or the other seems not to have survived in the archives or in the memories of witnesses.[2]

Copies: Not found.

Reproductions: Not found.

Listed: Not found.

1846 John Henry Brown

1847
Washington
Allon Bartlett

A map of the town of San Francisco. 1847.

Manuscript.

Note at base of map: "Chief Magistrate's Office. San Francisco, Feby. 22d, 1847. I hereby certify that this plan of the Town of San Francisco is the plan by which the titles have been given by the Alcaldes from the first location in the Town—and the numbers and names of lots and streets correspond with the records transferred by me. [Signed] Washn. A. Bartlett, Chief Magistrate."

>>><<<

THIS IS the "Alcalde map" of San Francisco, also known as "Bartlett's map" and "Buckalew's map," drawn late in December 1846 or in January 1847 and certified by Alcalde Bartlett on February 22, 1847, as the official map of the town.

After the occupation of California by United States forces and the raising of the flag at San Francisco on July 9, 1846, the town government was reorganized and Washington A. Bartlett was made alcalde or chief magistrate. One of the immediate problems of government had to do with the granting of town lots, a matter made urgent both by the increased demand for property in the place and the dire need to secure funds for the municipal treasury. In November 1846 Bartlett asked Jasper O'Farrell to undertake immediately a resurvey of the town, but meanwhile a revised copy of the old plan of Yerba Buena, by which lots were being issued, was made for the better protection of land titles. Quite possibly the map was also intended to be an official American restatement of the plan of the town to serve as a basis for O'Farrell's imminent work. The new map expanded the area of the old plan, bringing the number of lots to 360, and made it the second enlargement of the Vioget survey of 1839.

According to George Hyde, the map was made between December 15, 1846, and January 20, 1847, while he acted as temporary alcalde during Bartlett's absence in the interior, and he said that it was made by Benjamin

From a photograph, in the California State Library, of the original map.

Map No. 36

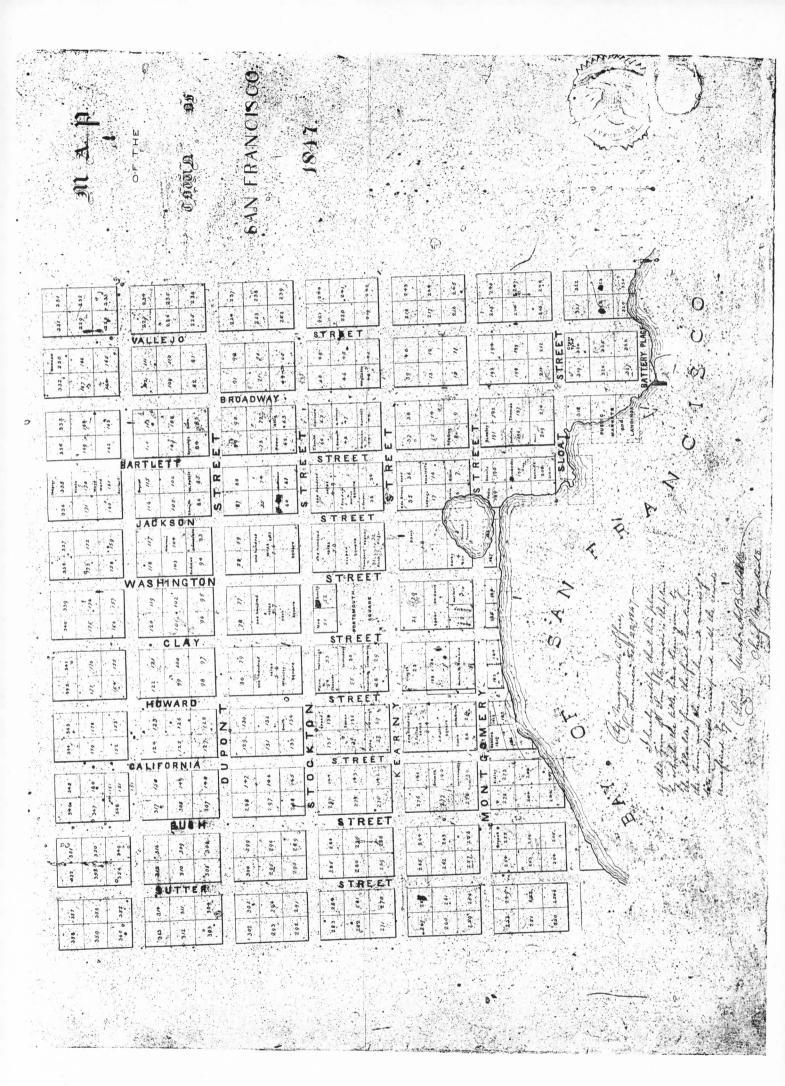

From the copy owned by the *Title Insurance and Guarantee Company, San Francisco.*

R. Buckalew, a local jeweler and publisher. After Bartlett's return to town in mid-January, he gave the map a title, named the streets, and on February 22, 1847, certified it as the official map of San Francisco. It embraced the area from the waterfront (including one block on Battery Street) north to present-day Green Street, west to Mason, and south to Sutter, though the names of the streets did not follow the order finally adopted. According to Bartlett's testimony the map was copied from the unnamed plan on coarse brown paper which he had received with the town archives from José de Jesús Noé, presumably the old map of *circa* 1843. It was still in existence in 1867, preserved in the Recorder's office in San Francisco, and was probably destroyed in the fire of 1906.[1]

Of the copies noted below, the photograph of the original which was certified as a true copy in 1867, does not show the streets intersecting at right angles, while on the certified copy of 1852, which is apparently a redrawing of the 1847 map, the blocks appear as squares. Since O'Farrell testified in 1860 that the Bartlett map was drawn with the streets at right angles,[2] it is possible that the appearance of the 1867 copy may have been the result of careless draughtsmanship in the original or of distortion brought about by its physical deterioration. It is interesting to note that O'Farrell stated that the Bartlett map was the first one of the city he ever saw.

Copies: Original map not extant. A small photograph of the original map is in the California State Library, certified as a true copy on November 30, 1867. Another photograph of a redrawing of the map, certified on October 26, 1852, is found as "Exhibit A" in the California Supreme Court archives, Sacramento (Case No. 2703. California. District court, 12th judicial district, *Paul Lestrade,* vs. *Frederick Barth,* Transcript of appeal). A third copy, dated May 18, 1857, is in the Recorder's office, San Francisco (Map book 2 A-B, p. 127, a reproduction of a tracing). A manuscript copy of the map, certified in 1857, is in the collection of the Title Insurance and Guaranty Company, San Francisco.

Reproductions: The 1867 photograph is reproduced in Eldredge, *The beginnings of San Francisco,* 1912, v. 2, p. 514. The 1852 copy is published in the *Pacific historical review,* v. 16, p. 368, Nov. 1947.

Listed: Phillips, *California,* No. 220.

1847
Washington
Allon Bartlett

[37]

1847
Jasper O'Farrell

[Map of San Francisco. 1847.]¹

Manuscript.

THE MAP of the first modern survey of San Francisco, the earliest survey of the city made under the American regime.

Informality in matters of land titles and boundaries was characteristic of the Mexican period in California history, and it was no less true in regard to lands in San Francisco. The American occupation of California in July 1846 and the consequent increased demand for real property in the town made a greater strictness and accuracy in keeping land records essential. The existing maps by which lots had been and were still being issued did not coincide with street and property lines on the ground. Still following Vioget's plan of 1839, the streets in the city did not intersect at right angles, and there was no regularity in fencing lots. New lots were measured from old stakes, and O'Farrell declared that "no two streets or lots were parallel." In November 1846 Alcalde Washington A. Bartlett wrote to O'Farrell, stressing the urgency of a new survey: "I have the utmost desire to have the town surveyed at the earliest possible day—therefore I shall expect you at your earliest convenience as every day will make it more difficult to get matters arranged as I wish them regarding the streets and lots."²

Jasper O'Farrell, Dublin Irishman, came to Yerba Buena in 1843. He soon became engaged in his profession as engineer and surveyor and laid out a number of Mexican ranchos, including three of his own. He was Sutter's quartermaster in the Micheltorena campaign of 1845 but apparently played no active part in the affairs of the American occupation. Although he moved about the country a great deal, his headquarters seem to have been at San Rafael. On July 6, 1847, while engaged in the San Francisco survey (in June he had finished laying out the competing town of Francesca, or Benicia), he was appointed one of the official surveyors by the military governor, and he advertised in the contemporary *Californian* as a civil engineer and land surveyor, "Office, Portsmouth Square."

[98]

Later he entered politics, served as state senator from Sonoma county in 1859 and 1860, was nominated lieutenant-governor on the Democratic ticket in 1861, and was a member of the State Board of Harbor Commissioners from 1869 to 1871. When he died at San Francisco on November 16, 1875, the *Alta California* carried the following brief notice: "Hon. Jasper O'Farrell, ex-State Senator, and the first surveyor of San Francisco, died last night at nine o'clock"—this, no more, announced the end of the man who more than any other was responsible for the present outline of the city of San Francisco.[3]

O'Farrell's assignment to resurvey the town was of a two-fold character: to realign and organize the street and lot survey on the ground and to coordinate it with an enlarged map of the place which he was to make, based upon existing plans. In order to correct the unorthodox angles of the intersecting streets on the ground, it was necessary to shift the direction of the streets paralleling the waterfront two and a half degrees in a northeast and southwest direction. This result, known as "O'Farrell's swing," was obtained by swinging the line of the streets on a pivot anchored at the corner of Washington and Kearny, a change which altered most of the lot lines in the surveyed section and was much objected to by persons who "regarded their pickett fences so valuable." In one instance at least, O'Farrell testified, the movement of the lines was sufficient to leave a house and other improvements entirely out of the owner's lot. In so far as the making of a new map was concerned, no basic change in the old plan of the city was effected. In the southern and newer section of the city Market Street was laid out paralleling the road to the mission, and the lots in the addition were oriented in relation to it. In other respects the map was a projection of the old plan, enlarged on all sides.

On November 26, 1846, Bartlett first requested O'Farrell to survey the town,[4] and, during Bartlett's short absence from San Francisco in December 1846 and the following January, temporary alcalde George Hyde approved terms proposed by O'Farrell, again urging him to commence the survey immediately.[5] O'Farrell probably went to work at once, for he testified that he was employed in December to lay out the town. According to his statement the job was finished in July 1847, although his contract to survey lots continued during the administrations of alcaldes Bryant and Hyde.[6] Work in the town proper (north of Market Street) was apparently completed in May 1847, after which the beach and water lot survey was

1847
Jasper O'Farrell

[99]

1847
Jasper O'Farrell

made and some one hundred 100-vara lots were laid off in the section south of Market Street, near the Rincon.[7] Within the town north of Market Street the limits of the map were, roughly, from Francisco south to Geary and from "ordinary high water mark" west to Leavenworth and Jones; south of Market, the survey extended about to Brannan and from the Rincon to Fifth Street.

Copies: Original unknown; probably destroyed in the fire of 1906. A photostatic copy of a map with the title quoted above is found in Burns, *Centennial of the city of San Francisco,* [1915,] p. 19. It bears a certificate, dated June 28, 1849, that it is a copy of the "original map of San Francisco belonging to the town and formerly on file in the Office of the Alcalde"; except that this map also embraces the beach and water lot survey, its area represents very nearly the number of lots surveyed by O'Farrell by August 1847.[8]

Reproductions: Not found.

Listed: Not found.

[Map of the beach and water lots of San Francisco, A. D., 1847.][1]

1847
Jasper O'Farrell

Manuscript. [Perhaps also an engraved map.]

⇢⇢⇠⇠

A MAP of O'Farrell's survey of the lots in front of the town of San Francisco made prior to the public sale of lots in July 1847.

While Jasper O'Farrell was engaged in making his general survey of the town in 1847, a movement gained headway to lay off and sell the lots along the beach of Yerba Buena Cove. Although the area was at least partly submerged except at low water, this portion of the town had great potential value as it comprised the waterfront of the growing city and must in due time be covered or filled to deep water. Backed by speculative citizens and wharf-builders, the plan was also favored by town officials as a means of securing additional funds for the municipality.[2]

As California had not yet legally become a part of the United States by treaty with Mexico but was under American military control, representatives of neither nation could give valid titles to land. Notwithstanding, General S. W. Kearny, as military governor claiming authority from the President of the United States, issued a decree, dated March 10, 1847, granting and releasing to the town of San Francisco the desired plot, stipulating that it be divided into lots and auctioned for the benefit of the town.[3] The area included all the property in front of Montgomery Street to low water mark, and from the Rincon to Clark's Point, reserving government land. Edwin Bryant, alcalde, requested O'Farrell to make the waterfront survey prior to the public sale, and the work was probably done between mid-June and mid-July 1847. The auction, first announced for June 29, was postponed (probably because of the incomplete survey) until July and took place from July 20 to 23, 1847, when some 200 lots were sold.[4]

The original O'Farrell map was still in existence in the office of the sur-

1847
Jasper O'Farrell

veyor of San Francisco in 1864[5] and was presumably destroyed in 1906. It included the first 444 beach and water lots, and the limits of the map may be ascertained from any of the early successors to O'Farrell's map of the town. A wavy line on the map indicated ordinary high water mark.

Copies: No copy of the separate map of beach and water lots is known.

Reproductions: Not found.

Listed: Not found.

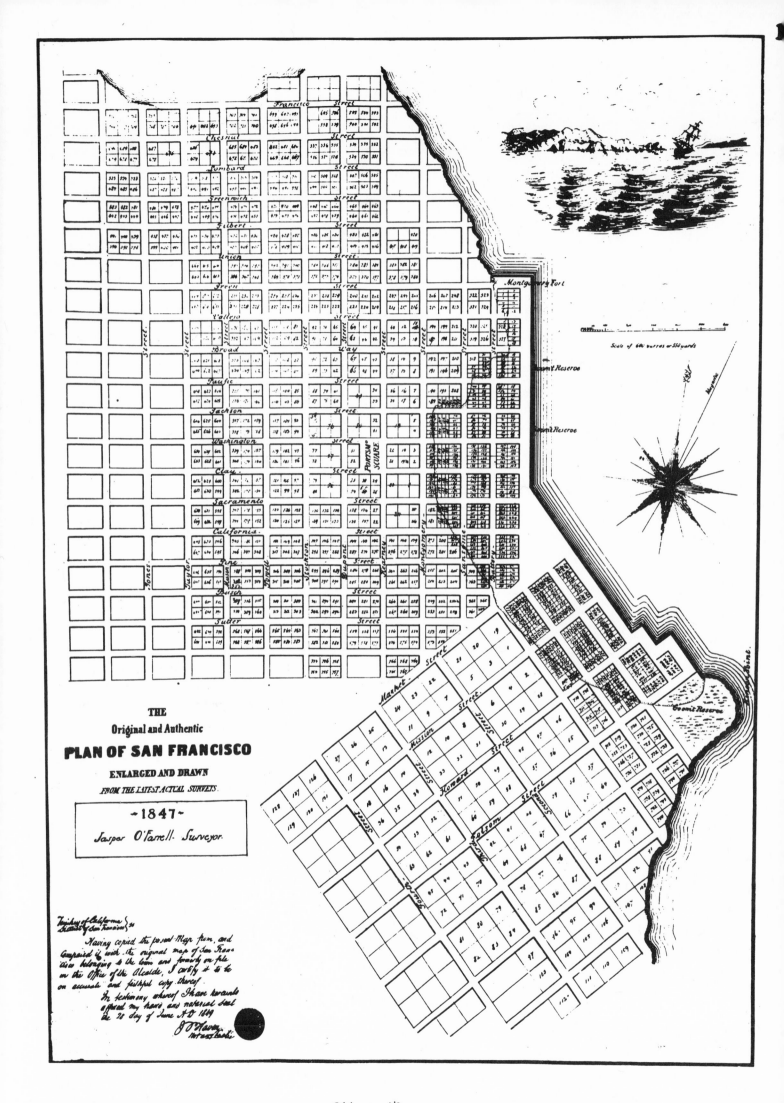

THE

Original and Authentic

PLAN OF SAN FRANCISCO

ENLARGED AND DRAWN

FROM THE LATEST ACTUAL SURVEYS

~1847~

Jaspar O'Farrell. Surveyor.

Scale of 600 varras or 550 yards

[The original and authentic plan of San Fran- 1847
cisco, enlarged and drawn from the latest actual   Jasper O'Farrell
surveys. 1847. Jasper O'Farrell, surveyor.]

Manuscript.

O'FARRELL's compiled map of San Francisco, combining the several surveys of the town made by him.

The 50-vara lots, spreading out from the original site of Yerba Buena, the 100-vara survey south of Market Street, and the water lots, situated in front of the town between the lines of low and high water, were laid out according to O'Farrell's contract by late in July 1847. Although the town continued to expand, and the number of surveyed lots to increase, O'Farrell brought together his partial maps into a single plan, probably during August 1847. This map, he testified in 1859, was a projection of the old Bartlett plan, enlarged upon all sides.[1] The plan, reported the *California Star* of August 27, 1847, represented the city as fronting upon the cove, and included both Telegraph Hill and the Rincon. The surveyed portion extended about three-quarters of a mile from north to south, and two miles from east to west, thus embracing approximately one and a half square miles. The plot was said to incorporate about 700 50-vara lots, some 150 of the 100-vara size, and about 450 beach and water lots. The earliest example of the map which has been observed shows 769 lots in the 50-vara class, about 130 of the 100-vara size, and 444 beach and water lots and is, therefore, nearly contemporary if not actually identical with the one described in August 1847.

O'Farrell's compiled map of 1847 was the culmination of twelve years of settlement and expansion which began with the arrival of William A. Richardson at Yerba Buena Cove in 1835. Much of the evolution can be traced in the map itself, and its engineered qualities contrast with the diseño-like appearance of the plans of 1835 and symbolize the great eco-

1847
Jasper O'Farrell

nomic, social, and political changes which had come to the region in that brief time.

Copies: The location of the original is unknown, but it is presumed to have disappeared in the San Francisco fire of 1906. A certified copy of the map with the title quoted above, made in 1849, may have escaped destruction at that time, for a photostat of it was in the possession of Thomas P. Burns and was presented by him to the Bancroft Library in 1935, where it is preserved.[2] The area of the map agrees closely with the description published in August 1847.

Reproductions: Not believed to have been published heretofore.

Listed: Not found.

NOTES

HISTORICAL ACCOUNT
& MAPS

ℂ Notes to the Historical Account

{ page 3 }

1. Wagner, *Spanish voyages to the northwest coast of America in the sixteenth century*, 1929, p. 72-93, 319-323, an account of the voyage, translation of documents, and bibliography. Wagner, *Juan Rodríguez Cabrillo, discoverer of the coast of California*, 1941. For a concise study of the early voyages to the north Pacific coast see also his *Cartography of the northwest coast of America to the year 1800*, 1937, v. 1.

2. Wagner, *Sir Francis Drake's voyage around the world*, 1926; "Nova Albion" and "Drake's anchorage," p. 135-169, sources, p. 238-403. Wagner concluded that Drake did not land at Drakes Bay but probably at Trinidad, Bodega, and perhaps other bays along the coast; *cf.* California historical society, *Drake's plate of brass*, 1937, and Fink and Polushkin, *Drake's plate of brass authenticated*, 1938.

3. Wagner, *Spanish voyages*, 1929, p. 139-153.

4. *Ibid.*, p. 154-167, 368-369.

5. Vizcaíno's voyage, *ibid.*, p. 168-282; bibliographic notes, p. 374-375, 378-392, 410-412.

6. By a cedula of August 19, 1606. (Wagner, *Spanish voyages*, 1929, p. 274-276.)

{ page 4 }

7. Bancroft, *California*, 1886-1890, v. 1, p. 110-116. Priestley, *José de Gálvez*, 1916, p. 234-254. Chapman, *The founding of Spanish California*, 1916, p. 68-91. Wagner suggests that perhaps Gálvez, upon finding Baja California not the land of wealth he had believed it to be, proposed the northern expedition to bolster his own reputation. (Wagner, *Cartography*, 1937, v. 1, p. 164.)

8. Rivera y Moncada left Velicatá March 24, arrived at San Diego May 14, 1769. Portolá completed the trip between May 15 and July 1, 1769. The *San Carlos* sailed from La Paz January 9, 1769, reached San Diego April 29. The *San Antonio* left San Lucas on February 15 and made San Diego on April 11 (or 14th, according to Crespí). See Bancroft, *California*, 1886-1890, v. 1, p. 126-135.

9. The party was comprised of Portolá, Fernando Rivera y Moncada in command of 20 soldiers, Sergeant José Francisco Ortega, Lieutenant Pedro Fages with 6 or 7 of his 25 Catalan volunteers, engineer Miguel Costansó, Juan Crespí, Francisco Gómez, 7 muleteers, 15 Lower California natives and 2 servants. (Bancroft, *op. cit.*, v. 1, p. 140-141.)

{ page 5 }

10. Following is the description of Drakes Bay by González Cabrera Bueno, whose sailing directions the expedition carried: "It is 38° ½ No. Lat. and is called San Francisco, with South and SE winds it is fit to ⚓ at the termination of the Beach, which makes an elbow at the SW part, and to the NE are Three white Cliffs very close to the Sea, which has a good entrance, without any breakers; within are Friendly Indians, and fresh water is got with great facility." (Translation from [Costansó], *An historical journal*, 1790, p. 47-48. Original text in González Cabrera Bueno, *Navegación especulativa, y práctica*, 1734, p. 302-303.)

11. For original accounts of the sighting of the Bay of the Farallones and the inland bay see Crespí, *Fray Juan Crespí*, 1927, p. 226-231, and Costansó's own diary, *The Portolá expedition of 1769-1770*, 1911, p. 263-267.

12. Crespí, *Fray Juan Crespí*, 1927, p. 230. The bay was labeled the "Estero de S. Francisco" on Costansó's *Carta reducida* of 1771; see catalog of maps, below, item No. 1.

13. The following contemporary accounts of the 1769 expedition are extant: (a) Mexico (Viceroyalty), *Estracto de noticias del puerto de Monterrey*, 1770, being the first official announcement of the expedition, two editions the same year. A reprint with English translation in Teggart, *The official account of the Portolá expedition of 1769-1770*, 1909. A more recent translation is found in Palóu, *Historical memoirs of New California*, 1926, v. 2, p. 301-306. (b) The longer official account promised in the *Estracto* is Costansó's *Diario histórico de los viages de mar y tierra*, 1770, MS.; published in an English translation by Dalrymple as [Costansó], *An historical journal of the expeditions by sea and land to the north of California*, 1790. The Spanish text, English translation, and a bibliographical note were issued as Costansó, *The narrative of the Portolá expedition of 1769-1770*, 1910, the same translation being printed again in Watson, *The Spanish occupation of California*, 1934, p. 24-63. (c) Costansó's personal diary was published as Costansó, *The Portolá expedition of 1769-1770*, 1911. (d) Crespí's diary was incorporated by Palóu in his *Noticias*, and is found in an English translation by Bolton in Palóu, *Historical memoirs*, 1926, v. 2, p. 109-260; and in Crespí, *Fray Juan Crespí*, 1927, p. 123-273. Crespí's correspondence regarding the expedition is in the latter volume. (e) Portolá's own diary was first published as the *Diary of Gaspar de Portolá during the California expedition of 1769-1770*, 1909. (f) A brief review of the expedition by Costansó is found in his *Noticias of the port of San Francisco . . . in the year 1772*, 1940, p. 15-22. (g) Pedro Fages' *Continuación y suplemento*, written in 1775, includes an account of the 1769 expedition, and an English translation by H. I. Priestley is found in Fages, *A historical, political, and natural description of California*, 1937.

{ page 6 }

14. Diary published as Fages, *Expedition to San Francisco Bay in 1770*, 1911. See also Fages to the Viceroy, in *ibid.*, p. 157.

15. See catalog of maps, below, item No. 2. Fages' order, dated in Mexico November 12, 1770, was received at Monterey May 21, 1771. (Bancroft, *California*, 1886-1890, v. 1, p. 175-176, 183.) Fages' diary of this expedition seems not to have been published. (Bolton in *California historical society quarterly*, 1931, v. 10, p. 212, note 7.) Translation of Crespí's diary in Palóu, *Historical memoirs*, 1926, v. 2, p. 329-354, and in Crespí, *Fray Juan Crespí*, 1927, p. 277-303. What is supposed to have been the first news of the undertaking to reach Mexico is a letter from Crespí to Palóu, sent by Costansó to Mexico and printed in Costansó, *Noticias of the port of San Francisco*, 1940, p. 2-6.

16. Palóu's report of the expedition in Palóu, *Historical memoirs*, 1926, v. 3, p. 248-308. See also his first report on the California missions in *ibid.*, v. 3, p. 234-235. Rivera's diary has not been published but is in the Archivo General de Indias. (Chapman, *Catalogue*, 1919, item 2761.) For Font's statement regarding Rivera's attitude toward San Francisco, see Bolton, *Anza's California expeditions*, 1930, v. 4, p. 225-227.

{ page 7 }

17. See catalog, map No. 3. Ayala's log of the voyage from San Blas to San Francisco and return remains unpublished except for a short summary, edited by E. J. Molera, in Eldredge, *The march of Portolá*, 1909, p. 52-58. A certified copy of the original diary is in the Bancroft Library, *Diario de navegación* (MS.). Cañizares' *Ynforme del reconocimto.*, and Ayala's report to the Viceroy are also found in Eldredge, *op. cit.*, p. 65-68, 59-61. A brief account of the expedition appears in Palóu, *Historical memoirs*, 1926, v. 4, p. 41-43; for other authorities see *ibid.*, p. 387-388, note 19.

It has often been stated that the *San Carlos* was carried into the bay by the tide, but Ayala's log does not so report it; see entry for August 5, 1775. Placing the first anchorage of the ship at Richardson Bay seems to best fit Ayala's description. (In Eldredge, *March of Portolá*, 1911, p. 56, the later presidio anchorage is specified, while Wagner's *Cartography*, 1937, v. 1, p. 179, and Chapman's *History of California, the Spanish period*, 1921, p. 279, both name North Beach as the place.) The launch probably spent the first night near the presidio anchorage.

18. Crespí's account is in Palóu, *Historical memoirs*, 1926, v. 3, p. 142-207, and in Crespí, *Fray Juan Crespí*, 1927, p. 307-366. See also Bancroft, *Northwest coast*, 1884, v. 1, p. 150-158; Wagner, *Cartography*, 1937, v. 1, p. 172-174.

{ *page 8* }

19. The *Santiago*, *Sonora*, and *San Carlos*, the latter headed for San Francisco, set out from San Blas together. Regarding Bodega's voyage see Bancroft, *California*, 1886-1890, v. 1, p. 241-244; Wagner, *Cartography*, 1937, v. 1, p. 175-179. Mourelle's account in Barrington, *Miscellanies*, 1781, p. 469-525; reprinted as Mourelle, *Voyage of the Sonora in the second Bucareli expedition*, 1920; see also LaPérouse, *A voyage round the world*, 1798, v. 1, p. 187-207.

20. Palóu, *Historical memoirs*, 1926, v. 4, p. 39-41. Bancroft, *California*, 1886-1890, v. 1, p. 247-248.

{ *page 9* }

21. Anza's diary of the 1775-1776 expedition from Mexico to California is in Bolton's *Anza's California expeditions*, 1930, v. 3, p. 1-200. Font's "long" and "short" diaries appear in *ibid.*, v. 3, p. 203-307, and in v. 4. The short diary was also published as Font, *The Anza expedition of 1775-1776; diary of Pedro Font*, 1913. A running account of Anza's two expeditions is given in Bolton, *An outpost of empire*, 1931. For Font's maps, see list below, Nos. 5-7.

22. Cañizares made a map showing the new findings; see below, map No. 4. Contemporary accounts of the founding of the presidio and mission are in Palóu, *Historical memoirs*, 1926, v. 4, p. 118-126, 132-138. For the explorations by Moraga and Quirós see *ibid.*, p. 127-131. Moraga's account in Bolton, *Anza's California expeditions*, 1930, v. 3, p. 409-420. Bolton tells the story in his *An outpost of empire*, 1931, p. 458-472. Chapman, *The founding of San Francisco*, 1917, p. 373-386, traces the development of Spanish official interest in San Francisco culminating in the settlement there in 1776.

{ *page 10* }

23. The resulting map was by Camacho; see catalog, map No. 8. For accounts of the voyage see Palóu, *Historical memoirs*, 1926, v. 4, p. 176-187; Wagner, *Cartography*, 1937, v. 1, p. 191-196 (includes bibliography; Wagner and Palóu differ occasionally in dates given).

24. Wagner, *Cartography*, 1937, v. 1, p. 197-198; and Historical society of southern California, *Quarterly publications*, v. 17, p. 135-138, Dec. 1935.

25. A royal cedula of May 10, 1780, ordered that voyages *de altura* be discontinued. (Bancroft, *Northwest coast*, 1884, v. 1, p. 173.) Regarding Cook's voyage, see Cook, *A voyage to the Pacific ocean*, 1784, 3 v. and atlas; and Wagner, *Cartography*, 1937, v. 1, p. 183-190.

26. Regarding the fur trade in the Pacific, see Ogden, *The California sea otter trade, 1784-1848*, 1941.

27. Wagner, *Cartography*, 1937, v. 1, p. 202-205. The vessels were the *Princesa* and *San Carlos*. Concerning the Nootka Sound controversy, the upshot of the 1789 expedition, see Wagner, *Cartography*, 1937, v. 1, p. 214-218, and Manning, *The Nootka Sound controversy*, 1905, p. 279-478.

28. Wagner, *op. cit.*, v. 1, p. 219-222. They commanded the *Concepción*, *San Carlos*, and *Princesa Real*, respectively.

29. *Ibid.*, v. 1, p. 225-230. Malaspina, *Viaje político-científico*, 1885. Summary of voyage and excerpts, in English translation, in Galbraith, *Malaspina's voyage around the world*, in *California historical society quarterly*, v. 3, p. 215-237, Oct. 1924. The entrance of San Francisco Bay was recognized in passing, but the *Descubierta* and *Atrevida* continued on to Monterey because of the fog.

30. The Galiano-Valdés and Caamaño voyages are treated in Wagner, *Cartography*, 1937, v. 1, p. 231-235. The atlas of the *Relación del viage hecho por las goletas Sutil y Mexicana*, 1802, in-

cludes a chart of the coast showing San Francisco, apparently from Arteaga's observations. An English translation of the account of the voyage was published as [Espinosa y Tello], *A Spanish voyage to Vancouver*, 1930. Caamaño's journal was published in English translation in the *British Columbia historical quarterly*, July and October 1938.

31. See Wagner, *The last Spanish exploration of the northwest coast*, in *California historical society quarterly*, Dec. 1931, v. 10, p. 314.

{ page 11 }

32. A map of San Francisco was included in the LaPérouse atlas; see No. 15 below. The official publication of the expedition was LaPérouse, *Voyage de la Pérouse autour du monde*, 1797. Also issued in an English edition, *A voyage round the world*, 1798, to which the following references are made: instructions regarding the California visit, v. 1, p. 73-74, 87-88; visit to Monterey and data regarding California, v. 2, p. 194-235. A curious apocryphal visit by members of the expedition to San Francisco Bay is reported in Dwinelle, *Colonial history of the city of San Francisco*, 3d ed., 1866, p. xiii.

33. For Vancouver's chart see catalog, No. 13. The official account of the voyage is Vancouver, *A voyage of discovery to the north Pacific Ocean and round the world*, 1798; directions to Vancouver, v. 1, p. xviii-xxii; Bodega Bay to San Francisco, v. 1, p. 428-432; San Francisco and Santa Clara, v. 2, p. 1-30; Nootka to San Francisco, v. 2, p. 431-435; jurisdiction of San Francisco, v. 2, p. 488. Bancroft concludes the anchorage was near North Beach (*California*, 1886-1890, v. 1, p. 702, note 12), but a comparison of the relative position of the anchorage shown on Vancouver's chart with the chart published by Dalrymple in 1790, which Wagner says was in Vancouver's possession (Wagner, *Cartography*, 1937, v. 1, p. 243) seems to prove that Vancouver dropped anchor first at Yerba Buena Cove.

{ page 12 }

34. Bancroft, *California*, 1886-1890, v. 1, p. 514.

35. Wagner, *The last Spanish exploration of the northwest coast and an attempt to colonize Bodega Bay*, in the *California historical society quarterly*, v. 10, p. 313-345, Dec. 1931.

36. *Ibid.*, p. 337-345. Bancroft, *California*, 1886-1890, v. 1, p. 515-517. The *Sutil* arrived at San Francisco on August 11, the *Aranzazu* on July 24, 1793.

37. Wagner, *The last Spanish exploration, op. cit.*, p. 334. Eliza's chart of San Francisco Bay apparently is not extant; he also made charts of Bodega, Monterey, and San Diego bays.

38. *Ibid.*, p. 331-332.

39. Vancouver, *Voyage*, 1798, v. 2, p. 431-434; observations at Bodega, p. 435-437.

40. *Ibid.*, v. 3, p. 322-324.

{ page 13 }

41. Langsdorff, *Voyages and travels in various parts of the world*, 1813, v. 2, p. 148-217. California material reprinted in Langsdorff's narrative of the *Rezánov voyage to Nueva California in 1806*, 1927.

{ page 14 }

42. Essig, *The Russian settlement at Ross*, 1933, p. 3-21. Bancroft, *California*, 1886-1890, v. 2, p. 296-299, 628-652.

43. The documents pertaining to the visit of the *Rurik* to San Francisco have been collected and published with English translations in Mahr, *The visit of the "Rurik" to San Francisco in 1816*, 1932.

44. Roquefeuil, *A voyage round the world between the years 1816-1818*, 1823, in *New voyages and travels* [n.d.]; see p. 24-27, 39-40, 106-110. Bancroft, *California*, 1886-1890, v. 2, p. 287-290.

{ *page 15* }

45. Corney, *Voyages in the northern Pacific*, 1896, p. 119-127. California portion reprinted as Corney, *The sack of Monterey*, 1940. See also Torchiana, *Story of the mission Santa Cruz*, 1933, p. 252-257; Bancroft, *California*, 1886-1890, v. 2, p. 220-249.

46. Regarding the effects of the revolutionary movement upon California, see Bancroft, *California*, 1886-1890, v. 2, p. 194-266; Chapman, *History of California*, 1921, p. 438-454.

47. Kotzebue, *A new voyage round the world*, 1830: San Francisco and the Sacramento river, v. 2, p. 73-77, 86-113, 136-150. Bancroft, *California*, 1886-1890, v. 2, p. 522-525.

{ *page 16* }

48. Morrell, *A narrative of four voyages to the South Sea*, 1832, p. 210-212. Bancroft, *op. cit.*, v. 3, p. 28.

49. For more complete data regarding the maps, see catalog of maps, below. For reissues of Cañizares' chart, see particularly 1781 – Cañizares (No. 9), published in Spain; 1789 – Dalrymple (No. 11), and 1790 – Dalrymple (No. 12), issued in London; 1797 – LaPérouse (No. 15), in Paris; and 1825 – Comisión hidrográfica (No. 18), in Mexico.

50. Vancouver, *Voyage*, 1798, v. 2, p. 15.

51. Bancroft, *California*, 1886-1890, v. 1, p. 551-552, 555.

{ *page 17* }

52. See, for example, Vancouver, *Voyage*, 1798, v. 2, p. 15; Langsdorff, *Voyages and travels*, 1813, v. 2, p. 198, 206; Beechey, *Narrative of a voyage*, 1831, v. 2, p. 5, 24-31; and Bancroft, *California*, 1886-1890, v. 2, p. 85, 91, 324, 328-329. Cook, *The conflict between the California Indians and white civilization*, II, 1943, p. 3-11, 49-55, lists punitive expeditions, 1800-1841.

53. Bancroft, *California*, 1886-1890, v. 2, p. 55.

54. Chapman, *History of California*, 1921, p. 423-424. The mythical third river tributary to the bay, the Jesús María, probably was born at this time. Moraga was gone from September 25 to October 23.

55. Chapman, *op. cit.*, p. 425-426. Bancroft, *op. cit.*, v. 2, p. 56.

56. Chapman, *op. cit.*, p. 426. Bancroft, *op. cit.*, v. 2, p. 321-323.

57. Chapman, *op. cit.*, p. 429-430. Duran, *Expedition on the Sacramento and San Joaquin rivers in 1817*, 1911.

58. For Ayala and Quirós expeditions, see above. Bodega y Quadra first surveyed and mapped Bodega Bay in 1775, an expedition not within the scope of this study.

{ *page 18* }

59. Bancroft, *California*, 1886-1890, v. 1, p. 516-517. Wagner, *The last Spanish exploration*, in the *California historical society quarterly*, v. 10, p. 337-345, Dec. 1931.

60. Ogden, *The California sea otter trade*, 1941, p. 58.

61. *Ibid.*, p. 59-60. Essig, *The Russian settlement at Ross*, in California historical society, *The Russians in California*, 1933, p. 4. Bancroft, *California*, 1886-1890, v. 2, p. 296-299. A base was also established on the Farallones.

Notes to the Historical Account

62. The 1810 expedition was against the Indians, the later ones to spy upon the Russians. Bancroft, *California*, 1886-1890, v. 2, p. 57, 300, 301, 303, 463-465, 506-507. Chapman, *History of California*, 1921, p. 424-425, 427.

63. Bancroft, *op. cit.*, v. 2, p. 329-331. Chapman, *op. cit.*, p. 430-431.

64. Route follows an interpretation of the Ordaz diary by Alice B. Maloney, in a letter to the writer, Oct. 17, 1943. Cf. Bancroft, *op. cit.*, v. 2, p. 445-449; and Chapman, *op. cit.*, p. 435-436. Copy of the Ordaz *Diario de la expedición de Don Luis Argüello al norte*, 1821, (MS) in the Bancroft Library.

65. Bancroft, *California*, 1886-1890, v. 2, p. 497-505. Translation of Altimira diary, *Journal of a mission founding expedition*, 1823, in *Hutchings' illustrated California magazine*, v. 5, p. 58-62, 115-118, Aug., Sept. 1860.

66. Bancroft, *op. cit.*, v. 3, p. 254-255.

{ *page 19* }

67. *Ibid.*, v. 3, p. 256-257.

68. *Ibid.*, v. 3, p. 293-295.

69. Beechey, *Narrative of a voyage to the Pacific and Beering's Strait*, 1831 (quarto ed.), v. 2, p. 1-87, 319-321; misinformation about the rivers, v. 2, p. 4-5. The California portion of the narrative with additional correspondence relating to the expedition has been published as Beechey, *An account of a visit to California, 1826-'27*, 1941.

{ *page 20* }

70. Ogden, *Hides and tallow*, in the *California historical society quarterly*, v. 6, p. 254-264, Sept. 1927. Ogden, *Boston hide droghers along California shores*, in *ibid.*, v. 8, p. 289-305, Dec. 1929.

71. Duhaut-Cilly, *Voyage autour du monde . . . 1826, 1827, 1828, 1829*, 1834-35. An English translation of the California material is in the *California historical society quarterly*, v. 8, p. 131-166, 214-250, 306-336, 1929. P. de Morineau, who may have visited California with Duhaut-Cilly, published a *Notice sur la Nouvelle-Californie* in the *Bulletin de la Société de géographie*, v. 16, p. 49-70, Aug. 1831, including a physical description of the "Port de San-Francisco;" see Bancroft, *California*, 1886-1890, v. 3, p. 408 and note 48.

{ *page 21* }

72. Sullivan, *Travels of Jedediah Smith*, 1934, p. 44-53. Sullivan, *Jedediah Smith, trader and trailbreaker*, 1936, p. 151-152. Dale, *The Ashley-Smith explorations*, 1941, p. 235-237, 239-241.

73. Maloney, *Hudson's Bay Company in California*, in the *Oregon historical quarterly*, v. 37, p. 9-23, March 1936. Hill, *Ewing Young in the fur trade of the far south west, 1822-1834*, in *ibid.*, v. 24, p. 1-35, March 1923. Bancroft, *California*, 1886-1890, v. 3, p. 285-395. Cleland, *Pathfinders*, 1929, p. 265-283. In 1835 the United States also tried to secure a foothold on the Pacific coast by purchasing San Francisco Bay from Mexico. (Cleland, *Early sentiment for annexation of California*, in the *Southwest historical quarterly*, v. 18, p. 12-16, July 1914.)

74. Dana, *Two years before the mast*, 1911, p. 281-291. An idea of the movements of one of the trading vessels during a stay on the coast is given by William D. Phelps: ". . . we were seven times at San Francisco, thirteen at Monterey, three at Santa Cruz, four at St. Louis, seventeen at Santa Barbara, seventeen at San Pedro, five at Refugio, and returned to our depot ten times, frequently anchoring at various other places along the shore. (Phelps, *Fore and aft*, 1871, p. 268.)

{ *page 22* }

75. Belcher, *Narrative of a voyage round the world*, 1843, v. 1, p. 114-134, 312-313, 317-318. Bancroft, *California*, 1886-1890, v. 4, p. 142-146.

76. Dupetit-Thouars, *Voyage autour du monde . . . 1836-1839*, 1840-1844, v. 2, p. 81, 101; v. 3, p. 330; v. 5, p. 179-182. Bancroft, *California*, 1886-1890, v. 4, p. 147-150. For chart see list below, No. 27.

77. Laplace, *Campagne de circumnavigation . . . 1837, 1838, 1839, et 1840*, 1841-1854, v. 6, p. 229-270. Bancroft, *California*, 1886-1890, v. 4, p. 152-155. Blue, *The report of Captain LaPlace*, in the *California historical society quarterly*, v. 18, p. 315-328, Dec. 1939.

{ *page 23* }

78. Zollinger, *Sutter, the man and his empire*, 1939, p. 63-66. Sutter followed the Feather River for a time and, like Moraga in 1808, believed it to be the main stream.

79. Duflot de Mofras, *Exploration du territoire de l'Oregon, des Californies et de la Mer Vermeille*, 1844, v. 1, p. 422-468. Duflot de Mofras, *Duflot de Mofras' travels on the Pacific coast*, 1937, v. 1, p. 224-249. Bancroft, *California*, 1886-1890, v. 4, p. 248-255.

80. Phelps, *Fore and aft*, 1871, p. 254-259. A number of other commercial voyages to the Pacific by Phelps are recounted in the volume.

{ *page 25* }

81. See list of maps, Nos. 24, 25. Wilkes, *Narrative of the United States exploring expedition*, 1845, v. 5, p. 151-256, 520-521. Wilkes, *Western America*, 1849, p. 42-45, including *A correct map . . . of California between Monterey and the prairie butes*. Bancroft, *California*, 1886-1890, v. 4, p. 240-248, includes a bibliography of publications of the expedition. A definitive list of the publications is available in Haskell, *The United States exploring expedition, 1838-1842*, 1942. For a criticism of Wilkes' report, see Eldredge, *The beginnings of San Francisco*, 1912, v. 1, p. 339-342.

82. Simpson, *Narrative of a journey round the world*, 1847, v. 1, p. 277-278, 282-340. Bancroft, *California*, 1886-1890, v. 4, p. 211-221.

83. Waseurts af Sandels, *A sojourn in California. By the King's Orphan*, 1945. Excerpts in the Society of California pioneers, *Quarterly*, v. 3, p. 58-98, June 1926. Part of the journal also appeared in Upham, *Notes of a voyage to California*, 1878, p. 537-562; and in the San Jose *Pioneer*, Jan. 11, 18, 25, Feb. 1, 1879. See also Bancroft, *California*, 1886-1890, v. 4, p. 345-346.

There were several earlier lone travelers in California. David Douglas and Thomas Coulter, English botanists, arrived in 1831 bent upon scientific errands; Douglas touched again at San Francisco in 1833. (Parry, *Early botanical explorers of the Pacific coast*, in *Overland monthly*, 2d ser., v. 2, p. 409-414, Oct. 1883. Bancroft, *California*, 1886-1890, v. 3, p. 403-407. Coulter, *Notes on Upper California*, in the *Journal of the Royal geographic society of London*, v. 5, p. 59-70, 1835, including a small map of California showing San Francisco Bay.) Two visitors who represented the rising interest of the United States in the Pacific were Hall J. Kelley, who arrived in California in 1834, and William A. Slacum, in 1837. (Kelley, *Mr. Kelley's memoir*, in U.S., 25th Cong., 3d sess., House report 101, supplementary report, p. 47-61. Slacum, [*Report*] in *ibid.*, p. 29-47.)

{ *page 26* }

84. Frémont, *Report of the exploring expedition*, 1845; the Buenaventura River and drainage of San Francisco Bay, p. 255-256. Frémont, *Memoirs of my life*, 1887; bay drainage, p. 363-364; Yerba Buena and San Francisco peninsula, Jan. 1846, p. 451-454. Concerning the 1846 visit, see also Nevins, *Frémont, the West's greatest explorer*, 1928, p. 250 ff. Of the general map in the *Report*, Frémont says "the bay of San Francisco is reduced from a copy of a manuscript map of a detailed survey in the possession of Mr. Sutter," probably a copy of Beechey's survey. (Frémont, *Report*, 1845, p. 321.)

85. Ringgold, *A series of charts and sailing directions*, 1851, p. 5-8. One general and five detailed charts make up the set. Ringgold's survey of San Pablo Bay, Carquinez Strait, and Suisun Bay

Notes to the Historical Account

was begun about July 1849 and completed in mid-August, when it was proposed to immediately extend it to Sacramento City. (San Francisco *Alta California*, Aug. 15, 1849, p. 2, col. 4.) In December the chart of Suisun was advertised to be ready "in a day or two" (*ibid.*, Dec. 6, 1849, p. 3, col. 4), but it was not offered for sale until the following March. (*Ibid.*, March 26, 1850, p. 2, col. 4.) By the middle of June 1850 the entire survey was said to be completed, and finished charts were to be made available "at the earliest moment." (*Ibid.*, June 18, 1850, p. 2, col. 2.) An earlier chart of Suisun Bay by James Blair, R. P. Hammond, and W. T. Sherman had been executed in April 1849 in connection with the development of the townsite of New York of the Pacific and was advertised in June. (*Ibid.*, April 26, 1849, p. 2, col. 2-3; June 21, 1849, p. 3, col. 2.)

Because serviceable charts of the bay were available in 1849 and 1850, the program of the U. S. Coast Survey on the Pacific coast was concerned at the beginning with more pressing assignments. First completed at San Francisco were minute surveys on the South Farallon, at Fort Point, Alcatraz, and Mare islands, needed to establish lighthouses and for purposes of defense. The general triangulation of the bay was then undertaken and the survey gradually extended. (U. S. Coast survey, *Report . . . for the year ending November 1850*, p. 11, 50. *Ibid.*, 1851, p. 84, 85-86.)

Notes to the Maps

{ *Map No.* 1, *page* 29 }

1. Bancroft, *California*, 1886-1890, v. 2, p. 768-769. Wagner, *Spanish Southwest*, 1937, p. 453. Priestley, *Miguel Costansó*, in the *Dictionary of American biography*, 1928-1944, v. 4, p. 460. Bolton, *Outpost of empire*, 1930, p. 50-52.

2. Wagner, *Spanish Southwest*, 1937, p. 449.

3. Mentioned in a letter from Costansó to Melchor de Peramás, dated at Mexico, October 9, 1772: "... we descried from the crest of a hill a very great Bay. From the Northwest side of it a point ran considerably out to Sea ... To the South-southwest of said Point were seen seven Farallones ... there were discovered to the North west, quarter west ... some White barrancas, precipitous to the Sea. There was also seen, toward the North, another great precipitous barranca; and by it entered a copious estuary, with two medium-sized Islets in the same mouth; all in the form shown by the adjoined small Plan, whose rough draft I made at that time." (Costansó, *Noticias of the port of San Francisco ... in the year 1772*, 1940, p. 16.)

4. The following reference is made by Pedro Fages: "... the port of San Francisco ... [is] situated in 37 degrees 35 minutes more or less, according to an observation taken on land near the port by Engineer Don Manuel [!] Costansó, who later made an excellent map of the peninsula, a faithful copy of which I have in my possession. On this map the port of San Francisco is situated in the latitude mentioned." (Fages, *A historical, political, and natural description of California*, 1937, p. 4.)

{ *Map No.* 2, *page* 32 }

1. Crespí, *Fray Juan Crespí*, 1927, p. xiii-lxi. Bolton, *Juan Crespí*, in the *Dictionary of American biography*, 1928-1944, v. 4, p. 539-540.

2. Lowery, *Descriptive list*, 1912, p. 367.

3. Crespí, *Fray Juan Crespí*, 1927, p. 303.

4. Chapman, *Catalogue of materials*, 1919, entry 1842; credited to Verger. An accompanying document (Chapman entry 2089) identifies it: "Acompaña copia de la representacion, diario y mapa que le pasó el Guardian del Colegio de San Fernando de Mexico correspondiente al nuevo descubrimto. del Puerto de S. Franco. en la Peninsula de Californias."

5. "Map of the port of San Francisco, March 1772, drawn by Fr. Rafael Verger from the observations of Fr. Juan Crespí." See Wagner, *Spanish southwest* (special illustrated ed.), 1924, p. 268 (legend on map).

6. Pedro Font remarked in his diary: "I occupied myself today [March 20, 1776] in copying the map of the port of San Francisco which my cousin, Fray Pablo Font, made in Mexico from the data in the diary kept by Fray Juan Crespí in that journey which he made with Captain Fages [1772]." (Bolton, *Anza's California expeditions*, 1930, v. 4, p. 310-311.)

{ *Map No.* 3, *page* 35 }

1. Bancroft, *California*, 1886-1890, v. 1, p. 132, note 13, p. 225, 329, 410, 444; v. 2, p. 741. Wagner, *Cartography*, 1937, v. 1, p. 179, 191, 192, 196, 217. Cañizares' report of reconnaissance at San Francisco is published in Eldredge, *March of Portolá*, 1909, p. 65-68; Ayala's recommendation to the viceroy, *ibid.*, p. 60.

2. Eldredge, *March of Portolá*, 1909, p. 68.

3. *Ibid.*, p. 59. Chapman, *Catalogue*, 1919, items 2985, 3028, 3033.

Notes to the Maps

4. This and the one preceding are apparently not complete or are reproductions of another example of the chart, for the scale at the base and the Farallones are not shown. These and the copy in Eldredge are facsimiles, that in Richman being redrawn.

{ *Map No.* 4, *page* 38 }

1. Palóu, *Historical memoirs*, 1926, v. 4, p. 129.

2. Wagner, *Cartography*, 1937, v. 2, p. 344, title 653.

3. See below, map No. 9.

{ *Map No.* 5, *page* 40 }

1. Scattered facts about Font may be found in Bolton, *Outpost of empire*, 1930. Bancroft, *California*, 1886-1890, see v. 3, p. 742 and index. Richman, *Pedro Font*, in the *Dictionary of American biography*, 1928–1944, v. 6, p. 497-498. Much about Font's personality may be learned from his diaries.

2. "[March 27, 1776] . . . I occupied myself a while in mapping, with a graphometer which Father Palóu loaned me, the mouth of the port, the Punta de Reyes, the Punta de Almejas, the Farallones which are out in the sea, and the length of the passage as far as the estuary . . .

"March 28.— . . . I again examined the mouth of the port and its configuration, using the graphometer, and I was able to sketch it, and the map is the one which I insert here at the end of this day." (Bolton, *Anza's California expeditions*, 1930, v. 4, p. 331, 341.)

3. Mentioned in Font's complete diary, in *ibid.*, v. 4, p. 337.

4. *Ibid.*, p. 331, 340.

5. *Ibid.*, p. vii.

6. For a bibliography of the Font diaries, see Bolton, *Anza's California expeditions*, 1930, v. 4, p. v; and Lowery, *Descriptive list*, 1912, p. 379-380.

{ *Map No.* 6, *page* 42 }

1. "Then a little further on we ascended a hill which is in a straight line with the mainland and the plain which runs toward a very thick grove of oaks and live oaks on the banks of the estuary, and is almost made into an island by two arms of the estuary. From there I mapped this grove and the two arms of the estuary, and I am inserting the map here on the back of this sheet." (Bolton, *Anza's California expeditions*, 1930, v. 4, p. 362.)

2. Included as an illustration in the text and not as a separate map, its exact position in the text being in the following sentence: "Afterwards we entered a plain in which we crossed two small [map here] arroyos without water." (Bolton, *Anza's California expeditions*, 1930, v. 4, p. 362.)

{ *Map No.* 7, *page* 43 }

1. The general map is not discussed here, San Francisco Bay being but a minute detail which is better represented in the separate Monterey-San Francisco map. See Wagner, *Cartography*, No. 658; Lowery, *Descriptive list*, No. 583.

2. Bolton, *Anza's California expeditions*, 1930, v. 4, p. 366. This question had been settled by Quirós and Cañizares in the fall of 1776.

3. *Ibid.*, v. 4, p. 396.

4. The map of this whole area could of course not be based entirely upon Font's personal observations. He stated that he had a copy of Bodega y Quadra's chart of Bodega Bay and a sketch map of San Francisco by the same authority. (Bolton, *Anza's California expeditions*, 1930, v. 4, p. 231.) Other sources were probably available to him in Mexico.

5. "Wednesday, April 10 [1776] — I busied myself by drawing a map of this journey which we made from Monterey to San Francisco and the Puerto Dulce, although I did not draw it very well, not being skilled at it, and because of the inconvenience under which I worked. . . . Thursday, April 11.— . . . Seeing the map which I made yesterday the reverend father president asked me to make one for him, and then Señor Ansa asked me to make still another one for him; so I was occupied in this work all day today, finishing the one which I made for the father president. Friday, April 12.— . . . Before noon I finished the map for Señor Ansa, and it turned out better than the two preceding ones, but not yet with all perfection, because of the inconvenience under which I worked. This sketch, drawn more to my satisfaction, is the plan or map which I insert here. It represents the entire journey which we made from Monterey to San Francisco and back, the route being indicated by dots." (Bolton, *Anza's California expeditions*, 1930, v. 4, p. 420-421.)

{ *Map No. 8, page* 45 }

1. Bancroft, *California*, 1886-1890, v. 1, p. 444; v. 2, p. 740. Wagner, *Cartography*, 1937, v. 1, p. 192, 195, 202, 215-216.

2. The charts are listed in Wagner, *Cartography*, 1937, v. 2, items 665, 668, 704, 707. For the chart of 1785, see below.

3. For an account of the 1779 Arteaga expedition, see Palóu, *Historical memoirs*, 1926, v. 4, p. 176-187; Wagner, *Cartography*, 1937, v. 1, p. 191-196. A manuscript report of the voyage by Mourelle in the William Andrews Clark Library (University of California, Los Angeles) comments but briefly on the San Francisco visit.

{ *Map No. 9, page* 47 }

1. Villavicencio also engraved a *Plano de la ciudad de México dividida en cuarteles*, which was printed in Mexico in 1782. Although not belonging in Palóu's *Life of Serra* (Watson, *The 1781 Cañizares map of San Francisco Bay*, in the *California historical society quarterly*, v. 13, p. 181, June 1934), the known copies of the 1781 chart have been found there; it is indicative that the book was also published in Mexico.

{ *Map No. 10, page* 48 }

1. For a discussion of the probable identity of the standard Spanish chart, see map No. 11 below.

{ *Map No. 11, page* 49 }

1. His other chart of San Francisco Bay is discussed below, map No. 12. Other Dalrymple west coast charts are noted in Wagner, *Cartography*, items 718-731, 745-747. For a brief biography of Dalrymple see the *Dictionary of national biography*, 1908-1909, v. 5, p. 402-403, and for a list of his published works consult the British Museum, *Catalogue of printed books*, 1881-1900, v. 17.

2. Wagner, *Cartography*, 1937, v. 1, p. 196; v. 2, p. 351 (No. 719).

3. Cox has received but scant notice in the literature pertaining to the early northwest coast trade. He is mentioned in Howay, *The Dixon-Meares controversy*, 1929, p. 35, 48, 49; Howay, *Early navigation of the Straits of Fuca*, in the *Oregon historical quarterly*, v. 12, p. 11, March 1911; Boit, *John Boit's log of the Columbia*, in *ibid.*, v. 22, p. 276, Dec. 1921. For charts and place names associated with Cox, see Wagner, *Cartography*, v. 2, p. 351 (No. 720), 356 (No. 783), 382, 445.

4. Wagner, *Cartography*, v. 2, p. 351 (No. 720).

{ *Map No. 12, page* 51 }

1. [Costansó], *Historical journal of expeditions by sea and land to the north of California*, 1790. The following note appears at p. ii: "I have added to the map of California by Don. Miguel

Costanso, the engineer of the expedition . . . a plate containing a plan of San Francisco, different from that formerly published, with a chart of part of the west coast of California from a Spanish MS; and also on the same plate I have given a plan and view of the Balle de Bandera. . . ."

{ *Map No.* 13, *page* 52 }

1. Wagner, *Cartography*, 1937, v. 1, p. 242-243.

2. Vancouver, *A voyage of discovery*, 1798, v. 1, p. 428-432; v. 2, p. 1-30, 431-435, 488; v. 3, p. 322-324. For a biography of Vancouver, see Godwin, *Vancouver, a life*, 1931.

3. Bancroft, *California*, 1886–1890, v. 1, p. 702, note 12.

{ *Map No.* 14, *page* 54 }

1. Bancroft, *California*, 1886-1890, v. 1, p. 515-517, 697-700. Bolton, *Guide*, 1913, p. 160-161. A sketch of Arrillaga's life is found in Bancroft, *California, op. cit.*, v. 2, p. 205-206.

{ *Map No.* 15, *page* 57 }

1. Dwinelle, in *The colonial history of the city of San Francisco* (3d ed., 1866, int. p. xiii), makes the following curious historical scoop: "It is well known that the ill-fated and gallant La Perouse, of the Royal French navy, touched at Monterey, in 1786, on his Exploring Expedition, before he sailed out into that great Pacific Ocean from which no tidings of him ever returned. While at Monterey he dispatched an expedition to the Port of San Francisco, which made a hydrographic chart of the Bay of San Francisco, which he sent to France, and which was published with the account of his explorations up to that point, and is therefore preserved to us. . . ." Dwinelle was also confused concerning the identity of the islands in the bay. For a brief biography of La-Pérouse, see Larousse, *Grand dictionnaire universal du XIXe siècle*, 1866-1890, v. 10, p. 180.

2. LaPérouse, *Voyage de la Pérouse*, 1798, v. 3, p. 380, 392.

3. See the discussion of the sources of the Dalrymple plan, above, map No. 11.

{ *Map No.* 16, *page* 59 }

1. Wagner, *Cartography*, 1937, v. 2, p. 355, item 770. Torres Lanzas, *Relación descriptiva*, 1900, item 487. For a similar map, see below, map No. 17.

{ *Map No.* 18, *page* 62 }

1. For additional information about the Spanish original, see above, maps Nos. 11, 15.

{ *Map No.* 19, *page* 63 }

1. Beechey, *Narrative of a voyage to the Pacific and Beering's Strait*, [quarto ed.] 1831, v. 2, p. 64; California portions of the voyage, v. 2, p. 1-87, 319-321. California material reprinted as Beechey, *An account of a visit to California*, [1941], with an introductory note regarding the personnel, purposes, and publications of the expedition, by Edith M. Coulter. Beechey's life is summarized in the *Dictionary of national biography*, 1908-1909, v. 2, p. 121-122.

2. Beechey, *Narrative, op. cit.*, v. 2, p. 4-5: "These rivers are named Jesus Maria, El Sacraménto, and Sán Joachin: the first, I was informed, takes a northerly direction, passes at the back of Bodega, and extends beyond Cape Mendocino. El Sacraménto trends to the N. E., and is said to have its rise in the rocky mountains near the source of the Columbia. The other, Sán Joachin, stretches to the southward, through the country of the Bolbones, and is divided from the S. E. arm of the harbour by a range of mountains."

3. The Martinez copies are discussed under map No. 20, below.

{ *Map No. 24, page 72* }

1. The official account of the expedition at San Francisco is found in Wilkes, *Narrative of the United States exploring expedition*, 1845, v. 5, p. 151-256, 520-521. Wilkes did not give a good report of his California experiences. For a short sketch of Wilkes' career, see the *Dictionary of American biography*, 1928-1944, v. 20, p. 216-217; a brief survey of the expedition and a definitive bibliography of its publications is available in Haskell, *The United States exploring expedition*, 1942.

{ *Map No. 26, page 75* }

1. Duflot de Mofras' acknowledgment to Beechey is in his *Exploration du territoire de l'Orégon*, 1844, v. 2, p. 482; his San Francisco visits are described in v. 1, p. 422-468. Among those who copied the Duflot de Mofras model were the compilers of two Russian editions (see above, map No. 19, *Additional notes*) and Carl Hartmann, whose *Baie und hafen von San Francisco* in his *Die wichtigsten häfen und rheden, sowie die goldregion von Californien*, 1849, was reproduced from the published edition of 1844. A brief review of the life of Duflot de Mofras and of his visit to Mexico and California prefaces *Duflot de Mofras' travels on the Pacific coast*, 1937, v. 1, p. xix-xxxiv.

{ *Map No. 27, page 77* }

1. For an account of the visit to California, see Dupetit-Thouars, *Voyage autour du monde . . . 1836-1839*, 1840-1844, v. 2, p. 81, 101; v. 3, p. 330; v. 5, p. 179-182. A biographical sketch appears in Larousse, *Grand dictionnaire universel du XIXe siècle*, 1866-1890, v. 6, p. 1406.

{ *Map No. 28, page 79* }

1. The *Carte détaillée du mouillage du Fort Ross et du Port de la Bodega ou Romanzoff dans la Nouvelle Californie, occupés par les Russes*. (53½ x 39 cm.) It is plate 17 in the atlas to Duflot de Mofras' *Exploration*. Regarding the 1841 manuscript map, see above, map No. 26.

{ *Map No. 30, page 83* }

1. Vancouver, *Voyage of discovery*, 1798, v. 2, p. 1. For a statement regarding Vancouver's place of anchorage, see above, map No. 13.

2. Richardson testified in 1853 concerning the anchorages at the presidio and at Yerba Buena; see U. S. District court, *The United States* vs. *José Y. Limantour*, 1857, v. 1, p. 22-23. See also Hittell, *California*, 1898, v. 2, p. 202.

3. For biographical information see Bancroft, *California*, 1886-1890, v. 5, p. 694, and his own deposition in U. S. District court, *The United States* vs. *José Y. Limantour*, op. cit., p. 21-35. His testimony in the San Francisco pueblo lands case is also biographical in nature; see U. S. Board of land commissioners, *Documents, depositions and brief*, 1854, p. 24-33, and *The Pioneer; or, California monthly magazine*, v. 1, p. 193-196, April 1854. Richardson, *Testimony of William A. Richardson . . . in private land grant cases of California*, compiled by J. N. Bowman, includes much of this data. A daughter of W. A. Richardson, Mariana Richardson Torres, remarked that her father came to California "to sound the Port of San Francisco and open its harbor to the world." (Torres, *Recollections of Mrs. Torres*, [n.d.,] *Addenda*, p. [1].)

4. For a brief history of the establishment of civil government at San Francisco, the fixing of the pueblo bounds, and the founding of Yerba Buena, consult Eldredge, *The beginnings of San Francisco*, 1912, v. 2, p. 500-505, and Bancroft, *California*, 1886-1890, v. 3, p. 702-708. Concerning the much discussed "Vallejo line" of the pueblo, see Dwinelle, *The colonial history of San Francisco*, 3d ed., 1866, *Addenda*, p. 116-119.

5. "Gov. Figueroa . . . asked me if there was any spot sufficient to lay off a small village or town. I told him there was one abreast of the anchorage where the vessels lay, a small place. He asked me the extent, and wished me to give him a small sketch of it, which I did, stating the dimensions to the best of my knowledge of the clear spot. The sketch I made exhibited the land, and stated the extent to be about four hundred varas from the beach opposite the anchorage in a south-west direction; and the direction of the valley run [!] about north-west and south-east about twelve hundred yards. I told him there were very few springs and it was very scarce of water. The land above described, as exhibited by the sketch was clear of bushes." (U. S. Board of land commissioners, *Documents, depositions and brief*, 1854, p. 30; also in *The Pioneer; or, California monthly magazine*, v. 1, p. 196, April 1854.)

{ *Map No. 31, page 85* }

1. The governor's letter of approval was printed in U. S. Board of land commissioners, *Documents, depositions and brief*, 1854, p. 31, and in *The Pioneer; or, California monthly magazine*, v. 1, p. 196, April 1854. Richardson's testimony describing the laying out of the town and the making of the map is found in U. S. Board of land commissioners, *op. cit.*, p. 25, 26, 28; a similar statement in *The Pioneer*, v. 1, p. 193-196, April 1854. His testimony is also recorded in U. S. District court, *The United States* vs. *José Y. Limantour. Transcript of record*, 1857, v. 1, p. 26: "They measured off two hundred varas from the beach in a south-west direction, and then told me that I could select some place out of that limit . . . I told them I wished to go a little higher up . . . They then measured off another one hundred varas in the same direction . . . The magistrate, Don Francisco de Haro . . . then appointed the first sand hill to the southeast from where we were standing as the southeast boundary. He then went to the first sand hill with the Ayuntamiento, and I accompanied them, and he pointed to the direction in which the street must lay. . . . He commenced measuring, and measured off the three first one hundred vara lots . . . I selected the fifth one hundred vara lot from the starting point. He measured off no more in that direction but declared all the land in that direction, on that line to the waters of the Bay [North Beach] as the northwest boundary for the small settlement of Yerba Buena, and at the same time laid off the street in that same direction, which he called Calle de la Fundación, and measured two hundred varas more, from the southwest side of my lot, to the southwest, running into the hills, which he called the southwest boundary . . . The southeast [!] limits were three hundred varas from said street, in a southwest direction from the commencement of the street, and from the same street, in a northeast direction along the sand hills to the Bay. The borders of the water from that point all around towards the northwest, to what is now called the north beach, at the point where the southwest boundary came to the bay, formed the other boundary. The first two hundred varas measured off on the beach were reserved for government purposes."

2. Richardson's statement concerning copies of the map is found in U. S. Board of land commissioners, *Documents, depositions and brief*, 1854, p. 28-29, and in *The Pioneer; or, California monthly magazine*, v. 1, p. 194, 195, April 1854.

3. Statement by J. N. Bowman, Berkeley, California, to whom the writer is indebted for many suggestions regarding the maps of Yerba Buena. See Burns, *Centennial of the city of San Francisco*, 1935; and his *The oldest street in San Francisco*, in the *California historical society quarterly*, v. 13, p. 235-239, Sept. 1934. This may be the map said by Burns to have been made by Richardson in May 1835.

{ *Map No. 32, page 87* }

1. Bancroft, *California*, 1886-1890, v. 4, p. 710-711. Eldredge, *Beginnings of San Francisco*, 1912, v. 2, p. 700-701. A biographical sketch was published at the time of Leese's death in the San Francisco *Chronicle*, Feb. 2, 1892, p. 3, col. 4, indexed in the California State Library.

2. Map No. 31, above, the first official plan of the town.

3. The Leese-Vallejo grant is recorded in Wheeler, *Land titles in San Francisco*, 1852, Schedule A, p. 24; and the action of the U. S. Land Commission and the federal District Court is briefly summarized in Hoffman, *Report of land cases*, 1862, *Appendix*, p. 11. For a summary of the legal considerations involved in establishing the validity of the Leese title and a history of the case as it progressed through the California courts, see [*California reports*] (2d ed.), v. 3, p. 17-27; v. 18, p. 535-575; v. 20, p. 388-427; v. 28, p. 26-38; v. 29, p. 665-673. Some papers bearing upon the grant, mostly certified copies of 1850 and 1851, are found in the manuscript division of the Library of the University of California at Los Angeles. Upon an 1850 copy of the Leese-Vallejo petition of 1839, the boundaries of the lots are described as follows: "two lots of one hundred varas each, at the point known as the landing place of Yerba Buena, commencing these lots from the said point of the landing place at the margin of the sea, thence a north course to the little beach which is the front of the hundred varas, and for depth a west course one hundred varas towards the hill, also . . . twenty-five varas in the sea by the said point of the landing place for the construction of the wharf . . ."

⁌ *Map No. 33, page 90* ⁍

1. Wheeler, *Land titles in San Francisco*, 1852, p. 24.

2. For biographical data consult: Bancroft, *California*, 1886-1890, v. 5, p. 764. Barry and Patten, *Men and memories of San Francisco*, 1873, p. 210-212. U. S. Board of land commissioners, *Documents, depositions and brief*, 1854, p. 17-20. Vioget died either on October 22 or 26, 1855 (San Jose *Tribune*, Oct. 31, 1855, p. 3, col. 3, states it was the 22nd; the San Francisco *Bulletin*, Oct. 30, 1855, p. 3, col. 5, gives it as the 26th).

3. Richardson testified that he pointed out the landmarks and lines indicated on his map of 1835 to Vioget while he was working on the plan of 1839 (U. S. Board of land commissioners, *Documents, depositions and brief*, 1854, p. 29), but Vioget stated that in 1839 he had never heard of Richardson's map (*ibid.*, p. 19).

4. In regard to the court copy of the map Vioget testified in 1854: "This map is a copy not made by me, but is a copy of the map which I made and presented to Guerrero, with the exceptions of the dotted lines at the ends of the streets. It differs from my map also in the way in which the Plaza or Portsmouth Square is laid down. My map made said Plaza to embrace all the block between Clay and Washington, Dupont and Kearny, except two fifty vara lots on the west side of said block. This map only makes the Plaza embrace one fifty vara lot. This map also differs from mine in the east part. Montgomery street is not laid off here in the vicinity of the place called on this map 'Laguna,' as it was on my map. I laid off the blocks on Montgomery regularly as far north as Pacific street, with the exception of one fifty vara lot at the corner of Washington street. The vacant space on this map at the corner of Jackson and Montgomery, was laid out as forming a lot on my map." (*Ibid.*, p. 20.)

⁌ *Map No. 34, page 92* ⁍

1. For a list of the early grants within the town of Yerba Buena, consult Wheeler, *Land titles in San Francisco*, 1852, schedules A and E. The Sherreback lot, although dated 1843 on copies of Vioget's plan, is said by Wheeler to have been granted on May 1, 1842.

2. Bartlett's testimony is found in California. Supreme court, *Henry Rice, vs. James Cunningham. Transcript of appeal*, 1864, in *California supreme court records*, v. 27, p. 98-101. Brown's remarks are from his *Reminiscences and incidents of "The early days" of San Francisco*, 1933, p. 24-25. For Eldredge's statement see his *Beginnings of San Francisco*, 1912, v. 2, p. 512; if the map which he mentions was made in 1845, it was done in the latter part of the year, for the office of prefect was abolished on October 13, 1843, and not reëstablished until July 12, 1845. William H. Davis spoke of a survey of the town in 1844, but Bancroft believed it doubtful (Bancroft, *California*, 1886-1890, v. 4, p. 669). Leavenwourth and Short testified in California. Supreme court, *Henry Rice* vs. *James Cunningham, op. cit.*, p. 10. The inventory of 1845, handed by Alcalde José de la

Notes to the Maps

Cruz Sanchez to his successor, José de Jesús Noé, was printed in Spanish and English in *The Pioneer; or, California monthly magazine*, v. 1, p. 144-145, March 1854.

In addition to Bartlett's reference to Wilkes' expedition, another source credits members of the party with having run the line of the pueblo under Mariano G. Vallejo's supervision. That the "Vallejo line" was not the boundary of Yerba Buena need not be discussed here, but it was supposed to have been marked in 1834, not in 1841. (See Wilson, *The alcalde system of California*, in [*California reports*], v. 1, 1851, p. 565. Concerning the "Vallejo line," see Dwinelle, *The colonial history of San Francisco*, 3d ed., 1866, *Addenda*, p. 116-119.) No official hint is given in the report or map of San Francisco by the Wilkes expedition of a survey at Yerba Buena.

⸭ Map No. 35, page 94 ⸬

1. Brown's biography is related by himself in his *Reminiscences and incidents of "The early days" of San Francisco*, 1886; reprinted 1933. See also Bancroft, *California*, 1886-1890, v. 2, p. 732-733. The "first map of surveyed land" may be supposed to have been the one tentatively dated 1843 herein.

2. For the statement by Eldredge see his *Beginnings of San Francisco*, 1912, v. 2, p. 512. Brown described the map in his *Reminiscences*, 1933, p. 24-25. George Hyde's testimony is preserved in California Supreme court, *Henry Rice* vs. *James Cunningham. Transcript of appeal*, 1864, in *California Supreme court records*, v. 27, p. 73, 80, 85. Bartlett's statement appears in *ibid.*, p. 100-101, and the remarks of Leavenwourth and Short at p. 10.

⸭ Map No. 36, page 96 ⸬

1. Hyde's statements are from California Supreme court, *Henry Rice*, vs. *James Cunningham. Transcript of appeal*, 1864, in *California supreme court records*, v. 27, p. 80. Bancroft concluded that because O'Farrell was working on his survey early in 1847 it was he who made the Bartlett map. (Bancroft, *California*, 1886-1890, v. 5, p. 654-655.) Bartlett's testimony is in California. Supreme court, *Henry Rice*, vs. *James Cunningham, op. cit.*, v. 27, p. 98-101. More information about Bartlett's life may be had from Bancroft, *op. cit.*, v. 2, p. 712, and Hussey, *Identification of the author of "The Farthest West" letters*, in *California historical society quarterly*, Sept. 1937, v. 16, p. 213-214. The identity of the "old map" of Yerba Buena is discussed under the two previous entries, maps Nos. 34, 35. The name of Yerba Buena was officially changed to San Francisco by Alcalde Bartlett on January 30, 1847.

2. California. District court, 12th judicial district, *Paul Lestrade*, vs. *Frederick Barth. Transcript of appeal*, 1860, p. 16.

⸭ Map No. 37, page 98 ⸬

1. The title is quoted in a letter from James A. Hardie to the Alcalde of San Francisco, July 18, 1847, in Dwinelle, *Colonial history of the city of San Francisco*, 3d ed., 1866, *Addenda*, p. 259.

2. Society of California pioneers, *Quarterly*, v. 10, p. 98, 1933.

3. Bancroft, *California*, 1886-1890, v. 4, p. 757. Society of California pioneers, *Quarterly*, v. 10, p. 85-100, 1933. Swasey, *Early days and men of California*, 1891, p. 157-159. Prendergast, *Forgotten pioneers*, 1942, p. 66-79. Death notice in the San Francisco *Alta California*, Nov. 17, 1875, p. 1, col. 2.

4. Bartlett to O'Farrell, Nov. 26, 1846, in Society of California pioneers, *Quarterly*, v. 10, p. 98, 1933.

5. Hyde to O'Farrell, Dec. 24, 1846, in *ibid.*

6. O'Farrell's testimony regarding the survey, taken in 1859, is found in California. District court, 12th judicial district, *Paul Lestrade*, vs. *Frederick Barth. Transcript of appeal*, 1860, p. 16-17. Bryant's term was from March to June 1847; Hyde's followed, continuing until March 1848.

7. "I made a plan of the Town first in April or May 1847 and afterwards in July or June '47 a plan of the Beach and water lots." (O'Farrell, in California. District court, 12th judicial district. *Paul Lestrade*, vs. *Frederick Barth, op. cit.*, p. 16.) On March 6 and June 1, 1847, O'Farrell was paid by the city $1116 and $884 for surveying 50-vara lots; and on July 24, $1725 for the beach and water lot survey—of which latter amount $1250 was for the original survey of beach and water lots and $475 for a revision of this survey which O'Farrell deemed necessary. On July 24, $500 was paid for laying off one hundred 100-vara lots and an additional $150 for 36 100-vara lots. (Society of California pioneers, *Quarterly*, v. 10, p. 99, 1933.)

8. See map No. 39.

{ *Map No. 38, page 101* }

1. Title as quoted in James A. Hardie to the Alcalde of San Francisco, July 18, 1847, in Dwinelle, *The colonial history of the city of San Francisco*, 3d ed., 1866, *Addenda*, p. 259.

2. An initial public meeting urging this procedure was held on February 15, 1847. (San Francisco *California star*, Feb. 20, 1847, p. 2, col. 3.)

3. A contemporary statement concerning the status of titles to waterfront property in California appears in the *California star* of Jan. 16, 1847 (p. 2, col. 2-3). Kearny's proclamation and Alcalde Bryant's announcement of the sale in *ibid.*, March 20, 1847, p. 4, col. 2, and following issues. It is copied in Wheeler, *Land titles in San Francisco*, 1852, p. 19; in Soulé, *Annals of San Francisco*, 1855, p. 181; and elsewhere. W. H. Halleck interpreted Kearny's act as reserving government holdings in the area and releasing the remainder to the town, if the lots were within the town limits, not as an outright grant by the military government. (Bancroft, *California*, 1886-1890, v. 5, p. 653.)

4. Bryant was alcalde from March 1 to June 1, 1847, and his announcement of the sale was dated March 16. (*California star*, March 20, 1847, p. 4, col. 2.) O'Farrell completed his regular survey of the town about the end of May (see map above, No. 37), after which he seems to have laid out the town of Benicia, which was finished before June 12. (Prendergast, *Forgotten pioneers*, 1942, p. 76.) The 100-vara survey south of Market Street and the beach and water lot survey proceeded together, and an announcement in the *California star* of March 20, 1847, p. 2, col. 2, stated that an "engraved map" of the property in front of the town would be published shortly. The editor of the *Californian* reported on June 17, 1847, that "We have seen the map of the Beach and Water Lots, just finished by Mr. O'Farrell." (*Californian*, June 17, 1847, p. 3, col. 1.) On July 24 O'Farrell was paid $1725 for the beach and water lot survey, of which $1250 was for the survey as planned and $475 for a resurvey occasioned by alterations in the 100-vara section of the plan. (Society of California pioneers, *Quarterly*, v. 10, p. 99, 1933.) Concerning the survey and sale, see Bancroft, *California*, 1886-1890, v. 5, p. 653, and Soulé, *Annals of San Francisco*, 1855, p. 179-182. A short contemporary account of the sale in the *Californian*, July 24, 1847, p. 2, col. 2. List of purchasers and lots sold in Wheeler, *Land titles in San Francisco*, 1852, p. 72-89, Schedule F.

5. Dwinelle, *Colonial history of San Francisco*, 3d ed., 1866, *Addenda*, p. 264.

{ *Map No. 39, page 103* }

1. California. District court, 12th judicial district, *Paul Lestrade* vs. *Frederick Barth. Transcript of appeal*, 1860, p. 16-17. O'Farrell referred to the Bartlett or "Alcalde" map; see above, map No. 36.

2. In Burns, *Centennial of the city of San Francisco*, 1935, plate 19.

BIBLIOGRAPHY

ℭBibliography

ACADEMY OF PACIFIC COAST HISTORY. *Publications*. Berkeley, University of California press, 1909–1919. 4 v.

ALTAMIRA, JOSE. *Journal of a mission founding expedition north of San Francisco, in 1823*. In *Hutchings' illustrated California magazine*, v. 5, p. 58-62, 115-118, Aug., Sept. 1860.

ALVISO, VALENTIN. *Documentos para la historia de California, 1817– 1850*. (Manuscripts in the Bancroft Library.)

AYALA, MANUEL. *Diario de navegación que va á hacer el teniente de fragata de la real armada ... Dn. Juan Manuel de Ayala, 1775*. (Transcript of the original manuscript in the Bancroft Library.)

BANCROFT, HUBERT HOWE. *History of California*. San Francisco, The History company, 1886–1890. 7 v. (*Works* of Hubert Howe Bancroft, v. 18-24.)

BANCROFT, HUBERT HOWE. *History of the northwest coast*. San Francisco, The History company, 1884. 2 v. (*Works* of Hubert Howe Bancroft, v. 27-28.)

BARRINGTON, DAINES. *Miscellanies*. London, Printed by J. Nichols, 1781.

BARRY, THEODORE A., and PATTEN, B. A. *Men and memories of San Francisco in the "spring of '50."* San Francisco, A. L. Bancroft & Co., 1873.

BEECHEY, FREDERICK WILLIAM. *An account of a visit to California, 1826-'27 ... Introduction by Edith M. Coulter*. [San Francisco,] Printed at the Grabhorn press for the Book club of California, [1941].

BEECHEY, FREDERICK WILLIAM. *Narrative of a voyage to the Pacific and Beering's strait* [quarto]. London, Henry Colburn and Richard Bentley, 1831. 2 v.

BELCHER, EDWARD. *Narrative of a voyage round the world performed in Her Majesty's ship Sulphur during the years 1836–1842*. London, H. Colburn, 1843. 2 v.

BLUE, VERNE. *The report of Captain LaPlace*. In *California historical society quarterly*, v. 18, p. 315-328, Dec. 1939.

Bibliography

Boit, John. *John Boit's log of the Columbia, 1790–1793*. In *Oregon historical quarterly*, v. 22, p. 257-351, Dec. 1921.

Bolton, Herbert Eugene. *Anza's California expeditions*. Berkeley, University of California press, 1930. 5 v.

Bolton, Herbert Eugene. *Guide to the materials for the history of the United States in the principal archives of Mexico*. Washington, Carnegie institution of Washington, 1913.

Bolton, Herbert Eugene. *In the south San Joaquin ahead of Garcés*. In *California historical society quarterly*, v. 10, p. 211-219, Sept. 1931.

Bolton, Herbert Eugene. *Juan Crespí*. In *Dictionary of American biography*. New York, Charles Scribner's sons, 1930, v. 4, p. 539-540.

Bolton, Herbert Eugene. *Outpost of empire*. New York, A. A. Knopf, [c1931]. (First issued as v. 1 of his *Anza's California expeditions*.)

Brown, John Henry. *Reminiscences and incidents of "the early days" of San Francisco*. San Francisco, Mission journal pub. co., [1886]. Reprinted 1933 as *Reminiscences and incidents of early days of San Francisco (1845-50)*. San Francisco, The Grabhorn press, [1933].

Brown University. John Carter Brown Library. *San Francisco and California in 1776*. Providence, R. I., John Carter Brown library, 1911.

Burns, Thomas P. *Centennial of the City of San Francisco*. [1935]. (Typed manuscript in the Bancroft Library.)

Burns, Thomas P. *The oldest street in San Francisco*. In *California historical society quarterly*, v. 13, p. 235-239, Sept. 1934.

Caamano, Jacinto. *The journal of Jacinto Caamaño*. In *British Columbia historical quarterly*, v. 2, p. 189-222, 265-301, July, Oct. 1938.

California. Archives. *Provincial state papers*. (Manuscripts in the Bancroft Library.)

California. District Court, 12th Judicial District. *Paul Lestrade, appellant, vs. Frederick Barth, respondent. Transcript of appeal*. (Filed July 4, 1860.) (Manuscript in California Supreme court archives, Sacramento; case no. 2703.)

California. Supreme Court. *In the Supreme court of the state of California. Henry Rice, administrator of the estate of John Kittleman, de-*

ceased, appellant, vs. James Cunningham, et als., respondents. Transcript of appeal. San Francisco, Waters bros. & co., 1864.

CALIFORNIA. SUPREME COURT. *In the Supreme court of the state of California. Henry Rice ... vs. James Cunningham, et als. ... Brief of argument of appellant.* San Francisco, 1865.

California supreme court records. (A collection of printed transcripts in the California State Library.)

CALIFORNIA HISTORICAL SOCIETY. *Drake's plate of brass.* San Francisco, California historical society, 1937. (*Special publication,* No. 13.) (Also issued in the *California historical society quarterly,* v. 16, pt. 2, March 1937.)

CALIFORNIA HISTORICAL SOCIETY. *The Russians in California.* San Francisco, California historical society, 1933. (*Special publication,* no. 7.) (Also issued in the *California historical society quarterly,* v. 12, p. 189-276, Sept. 1933.)

California Historical Society Quarterly. v. 1– July 1922– San Francisco, California historical society, 1922-

[*California Reports.*] *Report of cases argued and determined in the Supreme court of the state of California.* San Francisco, 1851– v. 1–

California Star and Californian. (San Francisco.) 1847–1848.

Californian. (Monterey and San Francisco.) 1846–1848.

CHAPMAN, CHARLES EDWARD. *Catalogue of materials in the Archivo general de Indias for the history of the Pacific coast and the American southwest.* Berkeley, University of California press, 1919.

CHAPMAN, CHARLES EDWARD. *The founding of San Francisco.* In *The Pacific ocean in history.* New York, Macmillan co., 1917, p. 373-386.

CHAPMAN, CHARLES EDWARD. *The founding of Spanish California.* New York, Macmillan co., 1916.

CHAPMAN, CHARLES EDWARD. *A history of California; the Spanish period.* New York, Macmillan co., 1921.

CLELAND, ROBERT GLASS. *Early sentiment for annexation of California.* In *Southwest historical quarterly,* v. 18, p. 12-16, July 1914.

CLELAND, ROBERT GLASS. *Pathfinders.* Los Angeles, San Francisco, [etc.,] Powell publishing co. [1929].

Bibliography

CONTRA COSTA COUNTY. RECORDER. *Deed books*, v. 10. (Manuscripts in Contra Costa county court house, Martinez, California.)

COOK, JAMES. *A voyage to the Pacific ocean*. London, Printed by W. and A. Strahan for G. Nicol & T. Codell, 1784. 3 v. and atlas.

COOK, SHERBURN F. *The conflict between the California Indian and white civilization, ll*. Berkeley, University of California press, 1943. (*Ibero-Americana*, no. 22.)

CORNEY, PETER. *The sack of Monterey*. [San Francisco,] Book club of California, 1940. (*Pacific adventures*, no. 4.)

CORNEY, PETER. *Voyages in the northern Pacific*. Honolulu, T. G. Thrum, 1896.

COSTANSÓ, MIGUEL. *Diario histórico de los viages de mar y tierra hecho al norte de la California*. [México,] En la imprenta del superior gobierno, [1770].

[COSTANSÓ, MIGUEL.] *An historical journal of the expeditions by sea and land to the north of California; in 1768, 1769 and 1770*. London, Dalrymple, 1790.

COSTANSÓ, MIGUEL. *The narrative of the Portolá expedition of 1769–1770 . . .* edited by Adolph van Hamert-Engert . . . and Frederick J. Teggart. Berkeley, University of California, 1910. (*Publications* of the Academy of Pacific coast history, v. 1, no. 4.)

COSTANSÓ, MIGUEL. *Noticias of the port of San Francisco . . . In the year 1772*. [San Francisco, The Windsor press, 1940.]

COSTANSÓ, MIGUEL. *The Portolá expedition of 1769–1770 . . .* edited by Frederick J. Teggart. Berkeley, University of California, 1911. (*Publications* of the Academy of Pacific coast history, v. 2, no. 4.)

COULTER, THOMAS. *Notes on upper California*. In *Journal of the Royal geographic society of London*, v. 5, p. 59-70, 1835.

CRESPÍ, JUAN. *Fray Juan Crespí, missionary explorer on the Pacific coast, 1769–1774*, by Herbert Eugene Bolton. Berkeley, University of California press, 1927.

DALE, HARRISON CLIFFORD. *The Ashley-Smith explorations and the discovery of a central route to the Pacific, 1822–1829*. Cleveland, A. H. Clark co., 1918. (Revised edition, Glendale, A. H. Clark co., 1941.)

DANA, RICHARD HENRY. *Two years before the mast.* Boston and New York, Houghton Mifflin co., [c1911].

DAVIDSON, GEORGE. *Identification of Sir Francis Drake's anchorage on the coast of California in the year 1579.* San Francisco, California historical society, 1890.

DAVIS, WILLIAM HEATH. *Seventy-five years in California.* San Francisco, John Howell, 1929.

DUFLOT DE MOFRAS, EUGENE. *Duflot de Mofras' travels on the Pacific coast . . .* translated, edited and annotated by Marguerite Eyer Wilbur. Santa Ana, Calif., The Fine arts press, 1937. 2 v.

DUFLOT DE MOFRAS, EUGENE. *Exploration du territoire de l'Orégon, des Californies et de la Mer Vermeille.* Paris, Arthus Bertrand, 1844. 2 v. and atlas.

DUFLOT DE MOFRAS, EUGENE. *Mélanges.* 9 v. (Collection of manuscript and printed material in the Bancroft Library.)

DUHAUT-CILLY, AUGUSTE BERNARD. *Duhaut-Cilly's account of California in the years 1827–28,* translated from the French by Charles Franklin Carter. In *California historical society quarterly,* v. 8, p. 136-166, 219-250, 306-336, June-Dec., 1929.

DUHAUT-CILLY, AUGUSTE BERNARD. *Voyage autour du monde . . . pendant les années 1826, 1827, 1828 et 1829.* Paris, Chez Arthus Bertrand, 1834–1835. 2 v.

DUPETIT-THOUARS, ABEL AUBERT. *Voyage autour du monde, sur la frégate La Vénus pendant les années 1836–1839.* Paris, 1840–1844. 5 v. Accompanied by Tessan, U. de., *Atlas hydrographique.* Paris, 1845.

DURAN, NARCISO. *Expedition on the Sacramento and San Joaquin rivers in 1817 . . .* edited by Charles Edward Chapman. Berkeley, University of California, 1911. (*Publications* of the Academy of Pacific coast history, v. 2, no. 5.)

DWINELLE, JOHN WHIPPLE. *The colonial history of the city of San Francisco. 3d ed.* San Francisco, Towne & Bacon, 1866.

ELDREDGE, ZOETH SKINNER. *The beginnings of San Francisco.* San Francisco, Z. S. Eldredge, 1912. 2 v.

Bibliography

ELDREDGE, ZOETH SKINNER. *The march of Portolá and the discovery of the bay of San Francisco*. San Francisco, California promotion committee, 1909.

EMORY, WILLIAM HEMSLEY. *Notes of a military reconnoissance.* Washington, Wendell and Van Benthuysen, 1848. (U. S. 30th Cong., 1st sess., Senate ex. doc. 7.)

ENGELHARDT, CHARLES ANTHONY. *Missions and missionaries of California.* San Francisco, J. H. Barry co., 1908–1915. 4 v.

[ESPINOSA Y TELLO, JOSE.] *Atlas para el viage de las goletas Sutil y Mexicana al reconocimiento del estrecho de Juan de Fuca en 1792.* [Madrid, Imprenta real,] 1802. To accompany his *Relación del viage.* Madrid, [Imprenta real,] 1802. An English translation of the *Relación* appeared as *A Spanish voyage to Vancouver and the north-west coast of America.* London, Argonaut press, 1930.

ESSIG, EDWARD OLIVER. *The Russian settlement at Ross.* In *California historical society quarterly*, v. 12, p. 191-209, Sept. 1933. Also in California historical society. *The Russians in California.* San Francisco, 1933, p. 3-21.

FAGES, PEDRO. *Continuatión y suplemento a los dos impresos que de orden de este superior govierno han corrido.* México, 1775. (Transcript in the Bancroft Library.)

FAGES, PEDRO. *Expedition to San Francisco Bay in 1770* . . . edited by Herbert Eugene Bolton. Berkeley, University of California, 1911. (*Publications* of the Academy of Pacific coast history, vol. 2, no. 3.)

FAGES, PEDRO. *A historical, political, and natural description of California* . . . translated into English . . . by Herbert Ingram Priestley. Berkeley, University of California press, 1937.

FINK, COLIN GARFIELD, and POLUSHKIN, E. P. *Drake's plate of brass authenticated.* San Francisco, California historical society, 1938. (*Special publication*, no. 14.)

FONT, PEDRO. *The Anza expedition of 1775-1776* . . . edited by Frederick J. Teggart. Berkeley, University of California, 1913. (*Publications* of the Academy of Pacific coast history, v. 3, no. 1.)

FORBES, ALEXANDER. *California: a history of Upper and Lower California from their first discovery to the present time.* London, Smith, Elder

& co., 1839. Also published: San Francisco, T. C. Russell, 1919; and San Francisco, John Henry Nash, 1937.

FREMONT, JOHN CHARLES. *Memoirs of my life.* Chicago and New York, Belford, Clarke & co., 1887.

FREMONT, JOHN CHARLES. *Report of the exploring expedition to the Rocky Mountains in the year 1842 and to Oregon and north California in the years 1843–'44.* Washington, Gales and Seaton, 1845.

GALBRAITH, E. E. *Malaspina's voyage around the world.* In *California historical society quarterly*, v. 3, p. 215-237, Oct. 1924.

GODWIN, GEORGE STANLEY. *Vancouver, a life, 1757–1798.* New York, D. Appleton and co., 1931.

GONZALEZ CABRERA BUENO, JOSE. *Navegación especulativa, y práctica.* Manila, 1734.

HARTMANN, CARL. *Geographisch-statische beschreibung von Californien.* Weimar, B. F. Voigt, 1849. 2 v.

HARTMANN, CARL. *Die wichtigsten häfen und rheden, sowie die gold-region von Californien.* Weimar, B. F. Voigt, 1849.

HASKELL, DANIEL C. *The United States Exploring expedition, 1838–1842, and its publications, 1844–1874, a bibliography.* New York, New York Public library, 1942.

HILL, JOSEPH JOHN. *Ewing Young in the fur trade of the far southwest, 1822–1834.* In *Oregon historical quarterly*, v. 24, p. 1-35, March 1923.

HITTELL, JOHN SHERTZER. *A history of the city of San Francisco.* San Francisco, A. L. Bancroft & co., 1878.

HITTELL, THEODORE HENRY. *History of California.* San Francisco, N. J. Stone & co., 1898. 4 v.

HOWAY, F. W. *The Dixon-Meares controversy.* Toronto, The Ryerson press, c1929. (*Canadian historical studies.*)

HOWAY, F. W. *Early navigation of the Straits of Fuca.* In *Oregon historical quarterly*, v. 12, p. 1-32, March 1911.

Hutchings' illustrated California magazine. v. 1-5. July 1856–June 1861. San Francisco, Hutchings & Rosenfield [1856]-1861.

Bibliography

Index of maps of private land grant cases of California [in the U. S. District court archives, San Francisco]. 1941. (Typed manuscript in the Bancroft Library.)

KELLEY, HALL J. *Mr. Kelley's memoir* [on the Oregon country, dated Jan. 31, 1839]. [Washington, 1839.] U. S. 25th Cong., 3d sess., House rept. 101, supplement, p. 47-61. (Serial no. 351.)

KOTZEBUE, OTTO VON. *A new voyage round the world in the years 1823, 24, 25, and 26.* London, Henry Colburn and Richard Bentley, 1830. 2 v.

KOTZEBUE, OTTO VON. *A voyage of discovery into the South Sea and Beering's Straits, for the purpose of exploring a north-east passage.* London, Longman, Hurst, Rees, Orme and Brown, 1821. 3 v.

LANGE, HENRY. *Atlas von Nord-Amerika nach den neusten materielien.* Braunschweig, G. Westermann, 1854.

LANGSDORFF, GEORG HEINRICH VON. *Langsdorff's narrative of the Rezánov voyage to Nueva California in 1806.* San Francisco, T. C. Russell, 1927.

LANGSDORFF, GEORG HEINRICH VON. *Voyages and travels in various parts of the world during the years 1803, 1804, 1805, 1806, and 1807.* London, Printed for Henry Colburn, 1813–1814. 2 v.

LAPEROUSE, JEAN FRANCOIS GALAUP DE. *Voyage de la Pérouse autour du monde.* Paris, De l'imprimerie de la république, [1797]. 4 v. and atlas.

LAPEROUSE, JEAN FRANCOIS GALAUP DE. *A voyage round the world, performed in the years 1785, 1786, 1787, and 1788.* London, Printed for G. G. and J. Robinson, 1799. 2 v. and atlas. (Also published: London, J. Johnson, 1798. 3 v.)

LAPLACE, CYRILLE PIERRE THEODORE. *Campagne de circumnavigation de la frégate l'Artémise pendant les années 1837, 1838, 1839 et 1840.* Paris, A. Bertrand, 1841-1854. 6 v.

LOWERY, WOODBURY. *A descriptive list of maps of the Spanish possessions within the present limits of the United States, 1502-1820.* Washington, 1912.

MAHR, AUGUST CARL. *The visit of the "Rurik" to San Francisco in*

1816. Stanford University, Stanford university press, 1932. (University series: *History, economics and political science,* v. 2, no. 2.)

MALASPINA, ALEJANDRO. *Viaje político-científico alrededor del mundo . . . desde 1789 á 1794.* Madrid, Imprenta de la viúda é hijos de Abienzo, 1885.

MALONEY, ALICE BAY. *Hudson's Bay company in California.* In *Oregon historical quarterly,* v. 37, p. 9-23, March 1936.

MANNING, WILLIAM RAY. *The Nootka Sound controversy.* In American historical association. *Annual report,* 1904. Washington, 1905, p. 279-478.

MASTERS, R. S. *An historical review of the San Francisco exchange.* [San Francisco,] Pacific telephone and telegraph co., 1927.

MEXICO (VICEROYALTY). *Estracto de noticias del puerto de Monterrey.* [México, En la imprenta del superior govierno, 1770.]

MORINEAU, P. DE. *Notice sur la Nouvelle-Californie.* In *Bulletin de la Société géographie,* v. 16, p. 49-70, Paris, Aug. 1831.

MORRELL, BENJAMIN. *A narrative of four voyages . . . From the year 1822 to 1831.* New York, J. & J. Harper, 1832.

MOURELLE, FRANCISCO ANTONIO. *Voyage of the Sonora in the second Bucareli expedition to explore the northwest coast.* San Francisco, T. C. Russell, 1920.

Navigation, journal of the institute of. Los Angeles, 1946—

NEVINS, ALLAN. *Frémont, the west's greatest adventurer.* New York and London, Harper & brothers, 1928. 2 v.

OGDEN, ADELE. *Boston hides droghers along California shores.* In *California historical society quarterly,* v. 8, p. 289-305, Dec. 1929.

OGDEN, ADELE. *The California sea otter trade, 1784–1848.* Berkeley, University of California press, 1941.

OGDEN, ADELE. *Hides and tallow, McCulloch, Hartnell and company, 1822–1828.* In *California historical society quarterly,* v. 6, p. 254-264, Sept. 1927.

ORDAZ, BLAS. *Diario de la expedición de Don Luis Argüello al norte, 1821.* (Manuscript in the Bancroft Library.)

Bibliography

Oregon historical quarterly. v. 1– March 1900– Portland, Oregon historical society, 1900–

PALÓU, FRANCISCO. *Historical memoirs of New California* . . . edited by Herbert Eugene Bolton. Berkeley, University of California press, 1926. 4 v.

PALÓU, FRANCISCO. *Noticias de la Nueva California.* San Francisco, E. Bosqui y cía., 1874. 4 v.

PALÓU, FRANCISCO. *Relación histórica de la vida y apostólicas tareas del venerable padre Fray Junípero Serra.* México, En la imprenta de Don Felipe de Zúñiga y Ontiveros, 1787.

PANAMA PACIFIC HISTORICAL CONGRESS, 1915. *The Pacific ocean in history.* New York, The Macmillan co., 1917.

PARRY, C. C. *Early botanical explorers on the Pacific coast.* In *Overland monthly,* 2d series, v. 2, p. 409-414, Oct. 1883.

[PHELPS, WILLIAM D.] *Fore and aft. By "Webfoot."* Boston, Nichols & Hall, 1871.

PHILLIPS, PHILIP LEE. *A list of geographical atlases in the Library of Congress.* Washington, 1909–1920. 4 v.

PHILLIPS, PHILIP LEE. *A list of maps of America in the Library of Congress.* Washington, 1901.

PHILLIPS, PHILIP LEE. *A descriptive list of maps of California, and San Francisco, to 1865 inclusive, found in the Library of Congress.* (Typed manuscript in the State Library; similar list with varying map numbers in the Bancroft Library.)

The Pioneer; or, California monthly magazine. v. 1-4. Jan. 1854–Dec. 1855. San Francisco, W. H. Brooks & co., Le Count and Strong, 1854–1855.

PORTOLA, GASPAR DE. *Diary of Gaspar de Portolá during the California expedition of 1769–1770* . . . edited by Donald E. Smith . . . and Frederick J. Teggart. Berkeley, University of California, 1909. (*Publications* of the Academy of Pacific coast history, v. 1, no. 3.)

PRENDERGAST, THOMAS F. *Forgotten pioneers.* San Francisco, The Trade pressroom, 1942.

PRIESTLEY, HERBERT INGRAM. *José de Gálvez, visitor-general of New Spain.* Berkeley, University of California press, 1916. (*Publications in history*, v. 5.)

PRIESTLEY, HERBERT INGRAM. *Miguel Costansó.* In *Dictionary of American biography.* New York, Charles Scribner's sons, 1930, v. 4, p. 460.

RICHARDSON, J. *The zoology of Captain Beechey's voyage.* London, Bohn, 1839.

RICHARDSON, WILLIAM ANTONIO. *Testimony of William A. Richardson in private land grant cases of California.* Compiled by J. N. Bowman. 1943. (Typed manuscript in the Bancroft Library.)

RICHMAN, IRVING BERDINE. *California under Spain and Mexico, 1535–1847.* Boston and New York, Houghton Mifflin co., 1911.

RICHMAN, IRVING BERDINE. *Pedro Font.* In *Dictionary of American biography.* New York, Charles Scribner's sons, 1931, v. 6, p. 497-498.

RINGGOLD, CADWALADER. *A series of charts and sailing directions.* Washington, Printed by Jno. T. Towers, 1851.

ROQUEFEUIL, CAMILLE DE. *A voyage round the world between the years 1816–1818.* London, Printed for Sir Richard Phillips & co., 1823. In *New voyages and travels*, v. 9, [n.d.]. French edition published in Paris, 1823.

SANCHEZ, JOSE DE LA CRUZ. *Inventory of all the archives [of Yerba Buena] from the foundation of the ayuntamiento in 1835, to the end of the present year [1845].* In *The Pioneer; or, California monthly magazine*, v. 1, p. 142-144, March 1854. (In Spanish and English.)

SAN FRANCISCO *Alta California.* 1849–1891.

SAN FRANCISCO *Bulletin.* 1855–1929.

SAN JOSE *Pioneer.* 1877–1880, 1893–1901.

SAN JOSE *Tribune.* 1854–1862?

SIMPSON, GEORGE. *Narrative of a journey round the world, during the years 1841 and 1842.* London, H. Colburn, 1847. 2 v.

SLACUM, WILLIAM A. *Mr. Slacum's report [on Oregon and California, dated March 26, 1837].* [Washington, 1838.] U. S. 25th Cong., 3d sess., House rept. 101, supplement, p. 29-47; also in U. S. 25th Cong., 2d sess., Senate doc. 24, containing additional material. (Serial nos. 351, 314.)

Bibliography

SOCIETY OF CALIFORNIA PIONEERS, SAN FRANCISCO. *Quarterly of the Society of California pioneers.* v. 1– March 1924– San Francisco, The Society, 1924–

SOULE, FRANK, GIHON, J. H., and NISBET, JAMES. *The annals of San Francisco.* New York, D. Appleton & co., 1855.

SULLIVAN, MAURICE S. *Jedediah Smith, trader and trail breaker.* New York, Press of the pioneers, inc., 1936.

SULLIVAN, MAURICE S. *The travels of Jedediah Smith.* Santa Ana, Calif., The Fine arts press, 1934.

SWASEY, WILLIAM F. *The early days and men of California.* Oakland, Pacific press publishing co., 1891.

TEBIEN'KOV, M. D. [*Atlas of the northwest coast of America from Behring's Straits to Cape Corrientes and the Aleutian Islands.* St. Petersburg,] 1852. (Title in Russian.)

TEGGART, FREDERICK JOHN, ed. *The official account of the Portolá expedition of 1769–1770.* Berkeley, University of California, 1909. (*Publications* of the Academy of Pacific coast history, v. 1, no. 2.)

TESSEN, U. DE. *Atlas hydrographique.* See Dupetit-Thouars, Abel Aubert. *Voyage autour du monde.*

TORCHIANA, HENRY ALBERT. *Story of the mission Santa Cruz.* San Francisco, Paul Elder & co., 1933.

TORRES, MARIANA RICHARDSON. *Recollections of Mrs. Torres,* [n.d.] (Typed manuscript in the California State Library.)

TORRES LANZAS, PEDRO. *Relación descriptiva de los mapas, planos, &, de México y Floridas existentes en el Archivo general de Indias.* Sevilla, 1900. 2 v.

U. S. BOARD OF LAND COMMISSIONERS. *Documents, depositions and brief of law points raised thereon on behalf of the United States, in case number 280, before the U. S. Board of land commissioners. The city of San Francisco vs. the United States.* San Francisco, Commercial power presses, 1854.

U. S. COAST AND GEODETIC SURVEY. *Report . . . for the year ending November 1850.* Washington, 1851.

U. S. COAST AND GEODETIC SURVEY. *Report . . . for the year ending November 1851.* Washington, 1852.

U. S. District Court. California (Northern District). *The United States* v. *José Y. Limantour . . . Photographic exhibits, filed by the United States.* 1858. (Secretary of State of California, archives, Sacramento.)

U. S. District Court. California (Northern District). *The United States* vs. *José Y. Limantour.* [*No. 424.*] *Transcript of record . . . in case no. 548.* San Francisco, Whitton, Towne & co's. excelsior steam presses, 1857. (In *U. S.* vs. *Limantour*, v. 1, pt. 2, and v. 2, California State Library.)

U. S. Exploring Expedition. *United States exploring expedition during the years 1838, 1839, 1840, 1841, 1842 . . . Atlas of charts . . . From the surveys of the expedition* [to accompany v. 23 on *Hydrography*]. Philadelphia, C. Sherman, 1858. 2 v.

U. S. Exploring Expedition. *Narrative.* See Wilkes, Charles. *Narrative.*

Upham, Samuel C. *Notes of a voyage to California via Cape Horn.* Philadelphia, The Author, 1878.

Vancouver, George. *A voyage of discovery to the north Pacific ocean, and round the world . . . performed in the years 1790, 1791, 1792, 1793, 1794, and 1795.* London, Printed for G. G. and J. Robinson and J. Edwards, 1798. 3 v. and atlas.

Wagner, Henry Raup. *The cartography of the northwest coast of America to the year 1800.* Berkeley, University of California press, 1937. 2 v.

Wagner, Henry Raup. *An exploration of the coast of southern California in 1782* [Martínez]. Historical society of southern California. *Publications*, v. 17, p. 135-138, Dec. 1935.

Wagner, Henry Raup. *Juan Rodríguez Cabrillo.* San Francisco, California historical society, [c1941]. (*Special publication*, no. 17.)

Wagner, Henry Raup. *The last Spanish exploration of the northwest coast, and an attempt to colonize Bodega Bay.* In *California historical society quarterly*, v. 10, p. 313-345, Dec. 1931.

Wagner, Henry Raup. *Sir Francis Drake's voyage around the world.* San Francisco, John Howell, 1926.

Bibliography

WAGNER, HENRY RAUP. *The Spanish southwest, 1542–1794; an annotated bibliography*. Albuquerque, The Quivera society, 1937. 2 v. (*Publications*, v. 7.) (Also published: Berkeley, [J. J. Gillick & co., inc.,] 1924, including a special illustrated edition.)

WAGNER, HENRY RAUP. *Spanish voyages to the northwest coast of America in the sixteenth century*. San Francisco, California historical society, 1929. (*Special publication*, no. 4.)

WASEURTZ AF SANDELS, G. M. *A sojourn in California. By the King's Orphan*. San Francisco, The Book club of California, 1945. Printed from the manuscript in the library of the Society of California pioneers, San Francisco. Also printed in part in the following: Society of California pioneers. *Quarterly*, v. 3, p. 56-98, June 1926. San Jose *Pioneer*, Jan. 11, 18, 25, Feb. 1, 1879. Upham, *Notes of a voyage to California*, Philadelphia, 1878, p. 537-562.

WATSON, DOUGLAS SLOANE. *The 1781 Cañizares map of San Francisco Bay*. In *California historical society quarterly*, v. 13, p. 180-181, June 1934.

WATSON, DOUGLAS SLOANE. *The Spanish occupation of California*. San Francisco, The Grabhorn press, 1934.

WHEELER, ALFRED. *Land titles in San Francisco, and the laws affecting the same*. San Francisco, Alta California steam printing establishment, 1852.

WILKES, CHARLES. *Narrative of the United States exploring expedition during the years 1838, 1839, 1840, 1841, 1842*. Philadelphia, Lea and Blanchard, 1845. 5 v. and atlas.

WILKES, CHARLES. *Western America, including California and Oregon, with maps of those regions, and of "The Sacramento Valley."* Philadelphia, Lea and Blanchard, 1849.

WILKES, CHARLES. See also U. S. Exploring expedition.

WILSON, R. A. *The alcalde system of California*. In [*California reports.*] San Francisco, 1851, v. 1, p. 559-579.

WINSOR, JUSTIN. *Narrative and critical history of America*. Boston and New York, Houghton Mifflin & co. [c1889.] 8 v.

ZOLLINGER, JAMES PETER. *Sutter, the man and his empire*. New York and London, Oxford university press, 1939.

Addenda

Preamble

These addenda illustrate and describe two additional maps of San Francisco Bay made prior to 1847 that have come to light since the publication of my own research in 1950. The twenty-nine maps in that volume were numbered in chronological order. To maintain continuity the earlier of the two added here is given No. 3a and the second, although precedence for it is less certain, is assigned No. 3b. I thank Maurizio Martino Fine Books for reproducing illustrations of them, and the Bancroft Library and Public Records Office, Kew, for their cooperation in and consent to their reproduction.

As noted in my 1950 volume, Map No. 1, a coastal chart made by Costansó and dated October 30, 1770, was the first to acknowledge the existence of San Francisco Bay. The map used was from the first printed edition, and I noted that an earlier manuscript map, with a similar coast line but not depicting the bay, was known. Warren Heckrotte, a recognized expert and student of the maps of California and western North America, has informed me of a third Costansó manuscript map, differing from the others as follows:

"A manuscript chart by Costansó, bearing the same date and showing the bay, is in the Karpeles Manuscript Library, Santa Barbara. A description of it in Sotheby's catalog of May 3, 1988, states in part that it is 'in ink on paper, in four sheets (joined), watermarked fleur-de-lys and monogrammed IV; scales approximately 1:3,200,000, signed by Miguel Costansó . . . 835 x 835 mm, Mexico, October 30, 1770.'
"This manuscript map preceded the printed one you designated Map No. 1. It bears the same title but has small differences, among them the size and the repositioning of the words 'Puerto San Francisco' on the printed map so they seem more closely associated with the area of the San Francisco Bay, where those words on the manuscript now in Santa Barbara were associated with a small bay north of Point Reyes."

With this information from Heckrotte, it is now known that Costansó prepared at least three coastal charts based on sketches made by him in 1769 and from other sources. The first two are manuscripts, and the first of these does not show San Francisco Bay; the second shows and names it, and the third is the printed chart I listed and illustrated as No. 1.

Readers may be interested in a slightly later manuscript coastal chart showing and naming the bay, as it may have been drafted by Cañizares. Professor Herbert K. Beals of Oregon believes that this map, long held by the Library of Congress but only recently studied, probably was drafted by Cañizares in late 1774 or early 1775 at the request of Juan Pérez, leader of the first of three "Bucareli expeditions." The map may have come into the hands of American troops during the war with Mexico, and may be one whose existence Pérez hinted at in writings before his death in 1775. A report on this map, not examined critically for more than two centuries, so far as is known, is found in an article by Beals, assisted by Library of Congress staff member James Flatness, in *Terrae Incognitae, The Journal of the Society for the History of Discoveries* (Volume XXVII, 1995).

Finds such as theirs, and that of No. 3b by Alfred Newman (who was kind enough also to first contact me about this reprinting by Maurizio Martino Fine Books), are what keep the field of historical cartography dynamic and robust.

Neal Harlow
Los Angeles
June 1996

3a

Plano del Puerto de S^{n}. Francisco ... registrado por el paquebot de S.M. el S^{r}. Carlos al mando de D^{n}. Juan Manuel de Ayala Teniente de Fragara de la Real (Real) Armada.

36 x 54 cm. Colored manuscript.
31 features are identified by a table on the face of the map.
1776
José de Cañizares

Cañizares' first map (No. 3) is dated 1775. When he returned in 1776 to assist in establishing a new presidio at the port's entrance he renewed his explorations and is known to have prepared the chart presented here as No. 4. The two are quite different, the latter showing the locations of the new presidio and mission and extending further inland to incorporate recent information about the Sacramento-San Joaquin delta. No. 3a is similar to the 1775 plan but different in orientation. It apparently was prepared before the drafting of No. 4, as it does not include information about the inland rivers collected by a separate land party. For dating purposes, it does include a note that the presidio and mission, numbers 1 and 2 on it, were established in the month of October of the year 1776.

Copies: The original is at the Bancroft Library, University of California, Berkeley, call number G4362, S22, 1776, C4.
Reproductions: The Map Collector, Issue 63, Summer 1963.
Listed: Not found.

3b

Mapa del Puerto de Sⁿ. Francisco en el Nuebo Monterrey, que se halla en 37. grados y 13. minutos.
36 x 23 1/2 cm. Manuscript.
25 features are identified by a table on the map.
1776
José de Cañizares or his sources

This manuscript map is a fourth known plan of the bay by Cañizares or from his sources. It is the previously unknown "Spanish Ms." from which was made the English language map of 1790 (No. 12) by the British hydrographer, author, and publisher Alexander Dalrymple. It is inexplicably titled as shown above to include "en el Nuebo Monterrey," which Dalrymple corrected to read "Plan of Port San Francisco in New Albion." The outlines of this and No. 12 are essentially the same, although placement varies slightly. Dalrymple's place names, fewer in number, are almost exact translations, and the geographic representations of a mountain in the upper portions of both maps bear a striking similarity. The oval ink stamp above the mountain obviously is a later addition. The large island in the round central bay (called Bahia de Guadalupe ó Redondo on this plan and on Maps No. 3 and 3a, called Round Bay Guadalupe by Dalrymple, and now San Pablo Bay) was shown as a peninsula in Cañizare's 1776 chart (No. 4), which also has more refined shore lines. According to Alfred W. Newman, who found this map in 1991, that island and peninsula probably depict what is shown on later maps as Isla Plana (now Mare Island). This map, although drawn to a different scale, also has the same general outline of the bay as No. 4 and extends, as does the latter, inland to the river delta. Such details would appear to place the preparation of this plan in 1776, somewhere between No. 3a and No. 4. It is possible that it was made later by someone other than Cañizares who had knowledge of the findings of the 1776 exploration but did not have before him the chart illustrated here as No. 4. It is difficult to believe that Cañizares would have drafted this map after having made the greatly refined No. 4.

Copies: The original is at the Public Records Office, Kew, England, and identified there as Map 45 in State Papers 112/91.
Reproductions: The Map Collector, Issue 63, Summer 1993, p. 39.
Listed: Not found.